THE

Potted
Garden

THE
Potted
Garden

Daria Price Bowman

FRIEDMAN/FAIRFAX
PUBLISHERS

A FRIEDMAN/FAIRFAX BOOK

© 1997 by
Michael Friedman Publishing Group, Inc.

Library of Congress Cataloging-in-Publication data available upon request

ISBN 1-56799-508-X

Editor: Celeste Sollod
Art Director: Jeff Batzli
Designer: Jan Melchior
Photography Editors: Karen L. Barr/
Emilya Naymark

Color separations by
Bright Arts Graphics (S) Pte Ltd
Printed in China by LeefungAsco Printers Ltd.

For bulk purchases and special sales, please contact:
Friedman/Fairfax Publishers
Attention: Sales Department
15 West 26th Street
New York, New York 10010
212/685-6610   FAX 212/685-1307

Visit our website:
http://www.metrobooks.com

For my mother, Elizabeth T. Price,
who has always loved plants in pots

~

Sincere thanks are due my father, Carl Price, for serving as
my scientific sounding board as well as chief proofreader;
to Larry Keller of Hobensack & Keller for
generously sharing with me his vast knowledge
in the field of antique garden ornaments;
to Larry's assistant Joe Fizzano for his willingness
to show me piece after piece until I knew enough
to write about old pots and planters; to Steve Cooper
of Imperatore Nurseries, who graciously served as my
on-call horticulturist; to garden writer Charles Cresson,
who gave much-needed advice; to my husband,
Ernie, and daughters, Sam and Cassie, for their patience
and understanding; and to all the gardeners whose
imaginative and creative use of pots has given me the
inspiration I needed to write this book.

∽CONTENTS∾

Introduction

Gardens are the result
of a collaboration between
art and nature.

PENELOPE HOBHOUSE

W hat garden doesn't have room for the delightful contributions of plants in pots? And what gardener can't manage to create something beautiful with a little soil, a few plants, and a good, sound container?

It could be a ubiquitous group of red geraniums crowding the window box of a rustic chalet in the Bernese Alps. Or perhaps a few cheeky clusters of portulaca in terra-cotta pots decorating a Mexican courtyard. Maybe it's stately agapanthus lilies gracing an antique cast-iron urn in the conservatory of a grand English estate. Or it could be a venerable bonsai cypress in an ancient porcelain bowl on a New York City terrace.

Potted gardening draws on the same skills, knowledge, and inspirations that gardeners have always used when cultivating the ground. But potted gardens offer a different perspective—a horticultural environment within the confines of a terra-cotta pot or an old oak barrel.

Indoor gardeners with no more than a windowsill are every bit as fulfilled when their cymbidium orchids burst into bloom as is the owner of acres of gardens at the height of their borders' summer show.

A city dweller is able to transform a bare, dark, paved backyard into a colorful, lush oasis with feathery ferns in an antique lead cistern and a group of pink impatiens in ornamental pots. Bland doorways develop a regal bearing with the addition of potted evergreen sentries, and suburban poolsides lose their hard edge when a gay melange of potted annuals are scattered about.

Containers of plants are useful for covering up undesirable features like drainpipes, gas meters, and utility vents. And a specially built raised planting bed makes it possible for a wheelchair-bound person to till the earth.

Whatever form they take, plants in pots gratify the senses, offering beauty, flexibility, and variety to the gardener, indoors or out.

A windowsill lined with a treasured collection of small terra-cotta pots shines with the golden tones of forced miniature daffodils including 'Tête-à-Tête' and 'Minnow'.

⦃ A History of the Potted Garden ⦄

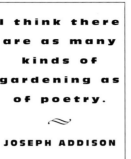

I think there are as many kinds of gardening as of poetry.

~

JOSEPH ADDISON

Men and women have been growing plants in pots for nearly as long as there have been pots to grow them in.

Outside the Minoan palace in Crete, archaeologists have uncovered remains of terra-cotta pots used for growing ornamental plants dating from 2100 B.C. Although there is no record of what was grown, historians suggest that potted roses, pomegranates, palms, irises, and madonna lilies adorned these early gardens.

In ancient Egypt, King Akhenaten and Queen Nefertiti grew pomegranate, date, and palm trees and lush vines in large tubs in the garden of their temple to the sun god. The legendary Hanging Gardens of Babylon, dating to the sixth century B.C., may have provided gardeners with the prototype of permanent planting beds on balconies and rooftop terraces.

Women planted lettuce, fennel, and barley seeds in clay pots to celebrate the festival of Adonis in ancient Greece. The seeds quickly sprouted, then withered and died, a symbol of the brief life of the handsome youth. Before long, ornamental plants were regularly placed in pots, and by the time of the Romans,

The Hanging Gardens of Babylon are considered among the Seven Wonders of the World. This legendary horticultural extravaganza adorned the levels of the Tower of Babylon, the palace built for King Nebuchadnezzar II in the sixth century B.C., and could be considered the prototype for raised-bed gardening.

ABOVE: *This ancient decorated storage jar was excavated from the Mallia site in Crete. Containers like this one might have been used to grow seeds or small fruit trees.*

OPPOSITE: *A mural inside the Casa del Frutteto in Pompeii, Italy, clearly depicts urns and planters in a garden setting.*

who built elaborate gardens, potted plants were displayed in public areas and on windowsills, balconies, and rooftops.

Starting around the ninth century, early followers of Islam built fabulous gardens, which served as examples of an earthly paradise while imparting a foretaste of life in heaven. These sensual places always featured pools of water and frequently held carefully restrained peach, apricot, plane, almond, and cypress trees planted in large tubs and arranged geometrically within the garden walls. Pots of roses also had an important place in Islamic gardens.

The Spanish Moors continued the Islamic tradition of dwarfing trees and planting them in tubs in the garden. There are fourteenth-century references to using pruned potted trees to protect the garden from north winds.

Tapestries, paintings, and illustrated manuscripts from the Middle Ages often depict garden scenes. If you look carefully, you'll frequently see raised beds where trees, shrubs, and flowers grow and bloom. In a fifteenth-century manuscript painting by Renaud de Montauban, a man and a woman sit within a fenced garden. Over her shoulder are carnations, a favorite of the day, blooming in a fluted pot and supported by tall stakes. There is also a pot on a pedestal holding a three-tiered topiary evergreen.

Throughout Europe, interest in plants grew as explorers traveled to southern shores, to the Far East, and to the New World, and horticultural treasures discovered abroad were brought back in tubs and pots. Since many of the plants were tender and would not have survived the cold climates of their new homes, the trees, shrubs, and flowering plants were potted up, sunk in the ground, and enveloped in elaborate frames. A painting of such a plant can be found in *Hortus Eystettensis*, a book published in 1613 in Nuremberg, Germany.

The art and architecture of the Italian Renaissance renewed interest in classical styles and brought a geometric approach to garden design. Huge palatial gardens featured square and circular patterns outlined with boxwood, bay, and myrtle hedges and were often punctuated by orange or lemon trees in massive earthenware pots.

In France, landscape architects, most notably André Le Nôtre, further stylized the Italian designs in vast parterres. Tender shrubs and trees, especially citrus, were imported and planted in enormous containers that were placed throughout the gardens. Records from Versailles, whose gardens Le Nôtre designed, show an order for 250,000 pots in 1686 and 1687.

LA PRÈTAIA

This wonderful lunette painting of the Villa Pretaia, a castle near Florence, gives us extraordinary details of the late-sixteenth-century gardens of Ferdinando de Medici, Grand Duke of Tuscany. Note the rows of orange or lemon trees in rounded terra-cotta pots on both sides of the rectangular pool.

Nowhere is the formal French style of garden design more beautifully defined than at Versailles. This painting by Jean Cotelle shows the water theater at the Grand Trianon. Note the elegantly placed urns planted with small trees, possibly oranges or lemons, that line the perimeter of the space.

To shelter the precious tender trees during the winter, huge glass houses called orangeries were built nearby. Later the orangeries would evolve into conservatories and ultimately greenhouses.

Le Nôtre also designed gardens for King Louis XIV at the Grand Trianon, a pink marble palace. He described the garden as "always filled with flowers which are changed every season in pots and one never sees a dead leaf, or a shrub not in bloom. It is necessary to change continuously more than two million pots...." The pots held flowers such as jasmine, lilies, carnations, tuberoses, hyacinths, and narcissi.

Beginning in the early seventeenth century, aristocratic European households commissioned the creation of ornate bronze vases and urns to grace their vast estates. Hand-crafted reproductions of these great pieces are still being made today by highly skilled artisans.

In eighteenth-century England, formal gardens became less fashionable, and a more naturalistic landscape became the favored style. But interest in horticultural discoveries continued to grow. Exotic and tender plants from around the world were raised in glass conservatories, often in ornate lead pots and tubs or artificial stone planters.

The Victorians of the next century were especially fond of exotic plants, and filled their conservatories with palms, lilies, orchids, and tropical plants in cast iron, stone, porcelain, and wicker planters. The rapid growth of a middle class, with its attendant surge in leisure time interests, spurred the manufacture of mass-produced cast iron, cement, and reconstituted stone garden ornaments including pots, planters, and urns.

"Bedding out," the practice of filling flower beds with masses of a few species of annual flowers, became the gardening trend. Public gardens and grand estates, in England and in the United States, where the style remained popular until the early twentieth century, would require thousands of plants in full bloom to fill the beds throughout the growing season. This was accomplished by growing vast numbers of potted plants in greenhouses, then transplanting them to the garden beds. Often, this task was undertaken several times during the growing season as different plants came into flower.

Pots continued to be used in garden schemes, but not often enough, at least according to Vita Sackville-West, one of the twentieth century's greatest gardeners. She wrote in one of her weekly gardening columns (published in London in *The Observer* from 1947 to 1961), "I wonder why people don't use pot plants more frequently...especially those people who have not a large garden and want to make use of every yard of space...."

TOP: *A hand-colored woodcut dating from about 1611 depicts a heavenly hand watering pots of flowers, possibly carnations.*

ABOVE: *Another woodcut represents "The Garden in April" in a series by H. Bol. Note the raised planting beds and the two flowerpots resting on the walkway.*

LEFT: *A trio of old copper planters, oxidized to a rich verdigris color, stand against the honey-colored stone of Tintinhull House in Somerset, England.*

A miniature garden grown in a collection of vintage teacups dresses up a windowsill in a high-rise apartment. Urban gardeners, the elderly, and the disabled can take advantage of miniature and dwarf varieties of plants and diminutive containers for manageable small gardens.

In another column she wrote, "I like the habit of pot gardening. It reminds me of the South—Italy, Spain, Provence, where pots of carnations and zinnias are stood carelessly about in a sunny courtyard or rising in tiers on the treads of an outside stair, dusty but oh how gay! I know it entails constant watering, but consider the convenience of being able to set down a smear of color just where you need it, in some corner where an earlier flower has gone off."

At Sissinghurst Castle, her home and the site of the extraordinary gardens she and her husband, Harold Nicolson, created in the countryside of Kent, England, Vita had pots of scented geraniums and verbena "standing about in a casual way round our front doors or in odd corners of the garden where you can tweak off a leaf and put it in your pocket or your buttonhole each morning."

Another of the century's greatest garden designers, Gertrude Jekyll, offered specific directions for using pots of plants to add accents of color and texture to the garden. In *Color Schemes for the Flower Garden*, published in 1908, she wrote, "Good groupings of smaller plants in pots is a form of ornament that might be made more use of in our gardens, especially where there are paved spaces near a house...."

In the twentieth century, gardening styles changed in response to changes in people's lifestyles. As homes became more modest and costs of labor increased, gardens became more personal, reflecting the tastes and interests of their owners. Gardening in pots matches the needs of apartment dwellers and suburbanites with small yards. But even those who garden in a majestic style find reasons to use containers in the garden.

At Dumbarton Oaks in Washington, D.C., the arbor garden, originally designed by Beatrix Ferrand, is filled with potted plants of all descriptions. C.Z. Guest, a garden writer and the owner of a grand estate on Long Island, grew tuberoses, topiaries, orchids, and camellias in containers to bring seasonal color and scent into her house. She also cultivated cut-leaf Japanese maples underplanted with creeping thyme in massive decorated planters, and lantana standards in simple terra-cotta pots.

At Tintinhull House, in Somerset, England, Penelope Hobhouse made extensive use of potted plants in her tenure as head gardener there. Throughout the estate, which is now a National Trust property, urns, pots, tubs, and planters filled with plants add color, scent, and interesting foliage shapes and textures to the garden.

⤳ Pots in Your Garden ⤳

Today, we garden in pots in innumerable ways. We turn our backs on winter with baskets of primroses and bowls of paperwhite narcissi. We grow herbs in coffee cans and on fire escapes. City terraces and rooftops are "greened" with potted trees, shrubs, and vines. Hanging baskets lush with fuchsias bring cheerful color to balconies, while window boxes full of geraniums and petunias signal the summer months in small towns.

Disabled gardeners grow vegetables in raised beds that are placed at just the right height for their wheelchairs. Meadow ponds, complete with lily pads and

> **The main purpose of a garden is to give its owner the best and highest kind of earthly pleasure.**
>
> ⤳
>
> **GERTRUDE JEKYLL**

colorful fish, are replicated in tubs or modern plastic pools.

Exotic mandevilla vines and gardenia standards grace backyard patios in even the most modest neighborhoods. Lovely old houses are made lovelier with the addition of artfully placed antique planters in their gardens.

In the following chapters, we'll look at the wealth of pots and containers as well as the limitless plants available to today's gardeners. And we'll see the beautiful ways people have interpreted, adapted, and created planting techniques and styles in potted gardens.

Blue tiles topping the walls of a raised bed and a colorful hand-painted pot repeat the blue theme of the tile-bedecked walkway in this San Francisco garden. Repeating themes of color, shapes, materials, or textures helps the gardener build a cohesive design in a lush garden that could otherwise become chaotic.

Chapter 1

POTS AND

The only limit to your
garden is at the boundaries of
your imagination.

~

THOMAS D. CHURCH

Extravagantly imaginative gardeners, or those
whose inclinations are oriented toward
the tried and true, have no difficulty finding
pots that fit their style of gardening.
A dilemma arises only in attempting to limit
one's selections to a few from the seemingly
endless array of pots, planters, jars,
bowls, boxes, barrels, vases, jugs, and
urns available to us.

In this chapter, we'll look at all the
pots gardeners use, from traditional
terra-cotta and classical urns to whimsical
boxes and troughs.

*Bold orange nasturtiums dominate a wall-hung planter
on a rustic wooden fence.*

CONTAINERS

∽ Terra-cotta and Ceramic Pots ∽

In meticulous garden diaries, Thomas Jefferson recorded his every horticultural activity in great detail. On April 29, 1809, for example, he wrote of planting fourteen "Koelreuteria paniculata aurea in 2 boxes & a pot, to wit 4 in the pot, 4 in the large box...."

In Jefferson's time, earthenware pots were readily available commercially, and, as Jefferson's garden diaries attest, he bought them in large quantities. Today, gardeners can buy exact reproductions of Jefferson's pots.

In early nineteenth-century England, large pottery factories began to manufacture high quality terra-cotta ornamental garden containers in colors ranging from buff to red. The tradition continues to this day. And from Impruneta, a small town in Tuscany, come exquisite terra-cotta pots as they have been crafted for twelve generations. These are exported for use by discriminating gardeners.

The term "terra-cotta" means baked earth. And that's exactly what these ubiquitous pots are. Usually handmade, they are fashioned from clay that is baked to a hard, brittle finish. Most terra-cotta pots have a warm, reddish-brown color, though variations in the pigment of the original clay can alter the tint of the container from deep rust to a color more closely approximating cream or white.

The use of terra-cotta pots offers gardeners reliable benefits: their porous nature allows more oxygen to reach the plants' root systems; germinating seeds as well as established roots will feel the sun's warmth sooner than in pots made of other materials; and excess water will quickly evaporate through the pot's surface.

However, the same porous characteristics allow the soil to dry quickly in hot or windy conditions, and can cause the roots to become overheated on especially scorching days.

The traditional flowerpots, with their tapered shape, wide collar, and large drainage hole, can be found in diminutive two-inch (5cm) forms or in sizes massive enough to hold a full-grown orange tree, with every size in between. In addition to the most typical form, terra-cotta is fashioned into an enormous array of styles and shapes, and is often enhanced with elegant, fanciful, and graceful ornamentation.

Terra-cotta pots come with fluted lips and rolled collars. They are formed into little cubes and sold with matching trays. There are bean pot, classical urn, and Ali Baba jar shapes. Rectangular planters, woven baskets with braided handles, contemporary bowls, pedestal urns, and distinctive strawberry jars are all made in terra-cotta.

One's taste, whether for the unadorned look or for elaborate decoration, is readily met with utterly smooth, plain surfaces, with intricate applied dec-

Though not originally designed to be used as garden ornaments, clay chimney pots serve that purpose with distinction. Shaped like tubes and open at the bottom, most chimney pots must be fitted with a "floor" in order to hold plants.

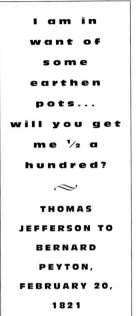

I am in want of some earthen pots... will you get me ½ a hundred?

∽

THOMAS JEFFERSON TO BERNARD PEYTON, FEBRUARY 20, 1821

oration, with ridges, grinning lions, rams' heads, swags, cupids, roping, garlands, classical details, and scrolled, checkerboard, basket-weave, shell, or stripe patterns.

When glazes are applied to terra-cotta pots, the pots lose their porous characteristics, retaining more moisture and not heating the interior as quickly. They also acquire a different aesthetic personality, taking perhaps a more aggressive stance in relation to the plants they house.

Gardeners have long found an enormous selection of ceramic pots suitable for all styles of gardening. Vita Sackville-West, for instance, was fond of a huge Ming dynasty jar, originally used to transport porcelains, which she kept in one of the gardens at Sissinghurst. She placed the blue-black jar in a bed of blue oxypetulum and plumbago, adding a pot full of morning glory

TOP: *Showy variegated* Aeonium *are paired with red primroses in a showy hand-crafted ceramic pot sporting a fanciful botanical theme.*

CENTER: *Sunflower 'Sunspot' in old terra-cotta pots enliven a blank brick wall.*

BOTTOM: *The bright yellow of these miniature 'Tête-à-Tête' daffodils presents a strong contrast to the deep blue of the glazed ceramic pot in the center of this unmatched grouping. The lone pansy and winterberry in plain weathered terra-cotta pots keep the design from being static.*

'Heavenly Blue' to "pour downwards in a symphony of different blues."

Other gardeners delight in delicate blue and white antique porcelains from China, which are perfect with white phalaenopsis orchids in an elegant conservatory. Inexpensive, brightly glazed cachepots work well with lush foliage plants in a greenhouse or a shaded corner of a patio.

A huge hand-painted urn from Thailand provides an appropriate home for a prized box topiary, while a simple earth-colored glazed Mexican bowl is ideal for a group of succulent hens-and-chicks. Bonsai gardeners will often select a simple glazed ceramic bowl for displaying their artful trees.

The single most important requirement for successful planting in terra-cotta or ceramic containers is adequate drainage.

A collection of Whichford pots, some mossy with age, await the gardener's choice of plants. Terra-cotta pots like these have been made from Warwickshire clay for generations. Styles range from strictly utilitarian to richly ornate with swags, lion heads, basket weave patterns, and medallions.

⮜ Stone and Reconstituted Stone ⮞

Stone is one of the oldest materials used to hold potted plants. The vast range of stone's natural colors and textures makes it an ideal medium for the artisans and craftsmen who have created beautiful stone garden ornaments for generations. Very early examples made by ancient Romans still surface from time to time, especially in spots where their spas were located.

A few examples of fine antique urns and vases of marble or granite still survive; usually, these are quickly bought by collectors with deep pockets. Exquisite examples of Vicenza and Istrian stone planters and urns command astronomical prices from noted antique dealers. Every once in a while, a rare vase of yellow or pink Bath stone or white Portland stonework will appear on the market, causing a flurry of interest.

The combination of stone and plants is especially beautiful, and fortunately one is not limited to rare antique examples to enhance the potted garden. Old stone sinks filled with herbs or colorful annuals can be found in farmyard gardens. New lava-rock troughs are the perfect stage for a garden of alpines or dwarf conifers. Elegant reproductions of early designs in reconstituted stone have found their way onto terraces and patios, where they play host to rose standards, dwarf peach trees, or mandevilla vines.

Among the most notable of reconstituted stones is sandstone, a pulverized stone mixed with an adhesive and formed in a mold, producing a thin-walled, soft yellow container noted for fine detail. Marble dust, another medium, is a powder made from crushed marble, which is liquefied and poured into molds to create good-looking milky gray pots. New granite planters cut by gifted artisans have a hard, smooth finish, generally with little detail and often with sleek, contemporary lines.

Stone and plant textures combine to create an intriguing area of the garden. Shrubs in pots provide balance in a planting scheme where the soil is inadequate for deep planting, where the plant that best enhances the grouping is too tender to be left outdoors in cold weather, or where another plant is planned but not yet installed. Having a few large potted specimens available for moving around gives the gardener the flexibility to be creative and innovative.

TOP: *Cascading plants are tucked into niches set within an ancient wall in Scotland. Many stone walls are designed with planting "pockets" in order to give the gardener the opportunity to drape the wall with blooms.*

BOTTOM: *Vivid red tulips 'Ballerina' make an intense statement in an ornate weathered stone urn in a Gloucestershire garden. Placing the urn atop a stone plinth gives the container and its plantings more height and importance.*

Set among hostas, peonies, astilbe, and delphiniums, a wide-mouthed urn atop an ornamented plinth adds height and weight to a garden grouping in Connecticut. Low-growing plants in the urn serve the design well. Taller plants would compete with the spiky delphiniums, making for a less pleasing composition.

Metal

Metal containers are among the most beautiful available to gardeners. At one time, Vita Sackville-West owned ten pairs of bronze vases, including an enormous pair modeled after the ones at Versailles and adorned with sphinxes, lions, acanthus leaves, and other elaborate ornamentation.

Monumental brass vases and urns made for royalty in the seventeenth century were enthusiastically reproduced to adorn the great country estates of later aristocracy. Today, bronze plant containers are most often found in public spaces, often interiors.

In the late seventeenth century and for about the next hundred years, garden ornaments, including vases, boxes, wellheads, lavabos, and urns, were often made of lead. The molten metal was poured into hand-crafted molds; then, after it had cooled and hardened, the lead was chased and finished. This process allowed for exquisite, fine detailing. Cupids, classical figures, garlands, and fruit were among the favorite themes.

Today, reproductions of eighteenth-century containers are made in England and the United States, with a few coming from France. Expensive and finely made, these pieces are treasured by their owners and make elegant and significant additions to any garden. Lead containers with-stand weather well; however, because lead is a soft metal, they may not stand up to very high temperatures, such as those found in desert regions.

Lead is a silver color when new. It is treated with acid solutions to darken it, and sometimes waxed. As it ages, it will develop a gray shading, eventually becoming a soft, powdery gray.

In the early part of the nineteenth century, manufacturers of garden ornaments began making their products in cast iron. A versatile medium, cast iron soon became so popular that foundries sprouted up throughout England and in the United States. Philadelphia became a major producer of cast iron, as did Baltimore and Boston.

Relatively inexpensive to produce, cast-iron garden containers were marketed in detailed catalogs, many of which have survived. True to the Victorians' love of intricate ornamentation, these urns, vases, bowls, and jardiniers were extravagantly adorned with floral designs—ferns, grapevines and clusters, medallions, cartouches, twining ivy, and rustic twig patterns. Cupids, classical and allegorical figures, and pastoral and hunting scenes were also popular.

Later, Art Deco designs gained favor. Loving-cup-shaped urns were among the preferred cast-iron garden ornaments of the period.

Wrought iron was another important medium for ornamental garden pieces. Though used mostly for making furniture, pergolas, and gazebos, wrought-iron plant stands and wall containers were crafted, too. The material lent itself particu-

Embellished with a cherub, a lead planter anchors massive begonia blooms and airy Helichrysum set at the edge of a paved area in a Dorset garden. Lead containers are enormously heavy, especially when filled with soil and plants. It's best to fill them in situ rather than attempting to move them once planted.

The graceful branches of this wall-mounted wrought-iron planter hold terra-cotta pots filled with ivy. Metal artisans fashion wrought iron into fanciful and ornate forms, ideal for enlivening a blank wall in the garden.

larly well to curving, scrolled patterns. Often planters were made to resemble climbing vines with round flowerpot holders added at intervals.

Metal wire wall planters and standing planters began to be made toward the end of the nineteenth century. Open, lacy, flowery patterns are reproduced today from the original French and English designs made nearly a hundred years ago.

Containers made from iron, whether cast, wrought, or wire, need a fair amount of maintenance, as they will rust. Most are painted black, white, or dark green, and they can be treated with rust-proofing products. Given a good wire-brushing, thorough cleaning, and a new coat of paint every year or so, iron containers will ably adorn your potted garden, and possibly your grandchildrens'.

RIGHT: *The pale blue of a wall niche is nicely echoed by the slightly darker blue of a large pot resting on its ledge. The cool dark green tones of the Boston fern* (Nephrolepsis exalta) *blur the distinction between the two blues.*

BELOW: *An eclectic collection of pots and plants is dominated by the vertical strength of a cement birdbath. The light gray of the cement repeats the color of the terrace in this California garden.*

✎ Cement ✎

I n the history of ornamental garden pots, cement is a relative newcomer, making its debut somewhere around the third quarter of the nineteenth century. Although mass-produced and eagerly bought up by enthusiastic gardeners newly elevated to the middle class, few early examples have survived. Cement, made from a blend of powdered stone, clay, resins, and aggregates, is relatively porous and will eventually deteriorate when exposed to the elements. Cement containers will serve for years, however, if given adequate care.

Their versatility and variety, not to mention their relative low cost, make cement planters enormously attractive to today's gardeners. Made throughout the world wherever labor costs are low, cement containers are fabricated in infinite styles, from sleek contemporary bowls to intricately ornamented urns.

While detailing is not as fine as might be found on containers of metal or stone, the shapes are often pleasingly refined. Quality ranges from downright crude to the accomplished work of true craftsmen. Most cement planters are gray, the exact shade dependent on the resins and aggregates found in the cement. The more porous cement planters will often take on a greenish tint if mosses and molds are allowed to grow on them.

Concrete pots and planters are especially suitable as containers for entrance gardens in urban areas, where their heft, along with the weight of soil and plant material, makes them unlikely targets for thieves. By the same token, their massive weight makes them inappropriate choices for balcony, deck, and some rooftop gardens, where weight is a significant consideration.

Plants of any type, from trees to tomatoes, will grow happily in a cement container. The key is to find a match between the plant's shape, texture, and size and the pot's styling. For example, a conical juniper or dwarf Alberta spruce will look especially elegant in a large container ornamented with garlands, lion or rams' heads, a basket weave pattern, or classical rosettes. A bright tumble of annuals might better be presented in a simple rolled-rim pot or one with minimal detail.

The walls of cement containers are thick and will maintain a relatively even temperature for roots. That same thickness reduces planting room in the pot's interior, a point to keep in mind.

A mossy urn serves as a stage for a bonsai evergreen. Note how the trunk bends as if it has been shaped by the wind. Among the most elegant of potted gardening forms, bonsai is an art form that originated in China around 350 B.C. Traditional bonsai is highly stylized and is judged by very specific, nearly ritualized rules. Dwarf varieties of shrubs and trees are further dwarfed with root pruning, pinching off shoots, structural cuts, and shaping with wires. Some bonsai trees are more than a hundred years old, yet are not more than a foot tall.

Wood

From rustic to regal, wooden containers for plants play a major role in the potted garden. Rough-hewn cow troughs, hollowed-out logs, rugged wooden buckets, wine crates, antique toolboxes, redwood window boxes, home-made wooden planters, and massive whiskey barrels enhance a country cottage garden, suburban patio, or eclectic city rooftop.

Vibrantly colored petunias, nicotianias, and nasturtiums tumbling from a wooden bucket, or a window box of bright geraniums and trailing lobelia look comforting and familiar in town and country gardens. Creative cooks enjoy the fresh flavor and convenience of culinary herbs tucked in a weathered wine crate close at hand on the back porch.

A big, old-fashioned whiskey barrel, cut in half, is an excellent choice for a simple water garden, providing enough room for a lily pad or two, a few aquatic grasses, and a lotus plant. If you have the time, you might add a few fish. Barrel-shaped tubs also make good homes for small ornamental trees and shrubs, fruit trees, teepees of morning glories or bush beans, and other flowering vines.

A formal garden setting will require more stylized wooden containers, with either contemporary or traditional lines.

Purple cabbage, scarlet nasturtiums, and orange marigolds occupy a rustic wooden trough. Wood planters are enormously versatile, working well with nearly endless combinations of plants.

Lengths of twig have been fashioned into a low-slung cart, making a charming container for purple and red petunias, pink impatiens and begonias, and trailing ivy. Though not sturdy, the cart will last through several seasons if stored in a dry place when not in use.

Large, cube-shaped tubs, called caisses Versailles, were the height of horticultural fashion in seventeenth-century formal French gardens like those at Versailles and Vaux-le-Vicomte. The elegant planters, holding orange and lemon trees, dotted the highly stylized landscapes, adding height, scent, and color to the scheme.

Today, these lovely planters are made with decorative finials, sometimes with raised or carved side panels, just as their predecessors were. They can also be manufactured with more contemporary styling. When used for permanent plantings, like shrubs, trees, or standards, they can be built with removable side panels to make for easier access to the root system for pruning.

White-painted formal wooden planters look their best when they are matched with tall, neatly pruned standards, full topiaries, dwarf trees, or neat shrubs. A pair of white-painted caisses Versailles fitted with standard bay, privet, or box, ivy topiary balls, or neatly trimmed cypress or juniper stand like elegant, well-dressed doormen at a front entrance.

In an area with full sun, you may want to paint the planters dark green or black to avoid bright glare.

A less formal setting might call for simple white cubes planted with a blowsy fuchsia standard, lavish standards of lantana or heliotrope, pretty lacecap hydrangeas, a variegated flowering maple, or dwarf fruit trees.

Like any container, wooden planters must have plenty of drainage holes in order for plants to survive. And you'll want to make sure your planters are deep enough for the plants you intend to use.

Unlike stone and man-made materials, untreated wood will rot after prolonged exposure to water. To extend the life of your containers and protect your plantings, select wood containers made from cedar and redwood, which are both resistant to rot. Hardware, paint, and garden stores sell preservatives which can be painted or sprayed inside and on the bottom of wooden containers. Select only preparations that are not toxic to plants or animals.

Raising wooden planters a few inches from the surface below them will also prevent draining water from pooling, which will eventually cause the wood to break down. If your containers don't already have "feet," use bricks, wooden blocks, trivets, or decorative terra-cotta or cement supports to keep the container bottom raised and dry.

Raised Beds and Permanent Structures

A circular raised bed constructed of multi-hued brick holds a crazy quilt of plants in chartreuse, yellow, pink, silver, burgundy, and green. The variegated hostas in pots on the brick terrace surrounding the bed repeat the multicolored theme.

Custom-made planters in innumerable configurations and sizes can be constructed to create planting beds for large paved spaces such as rooftops, courtyards, entranceways, or terraces. A simple rectangular raised bed in a small backyard makes the most of limited space using the principles of "square-foot gardening," in which a raised bed is divided into one-foot (30cm) squares, and each section is tightly planted with a different vegetable, herb, or flower. Tablelike wooden containers at wheelchair height are perfect for meeting the needs of disabled gardeners.

Raised beds and permanent planting structures are most often constructed of lumber, stone, brick, or reinforced concrete. The heavier materials can be used in the corners and along the walls of a courtyard, walled garden, paved area, or terrace to add planting space for trees, screening shrubs, windbreaks, vines, and underplantings of perennials, bulbs, and annuals. Architectural interest might be added to a nondescript area with built-in containers at several levels or planters with curving lines in an angular space.

Lighter materials for raised beds and planters are more suitable for a deck or rooftop garden where the ability of the space to support the weight is an important consideration.

The simplest permanent planting structure, and one that is raised only inches from ground level, is created by placing an old wooden ladder on a narrow strip of prepared ground. The ladder's rungs form small, neatly defined planting squares—ideal for an herb garden, a garden for a small child, or a whimsical ground-level container for annuals or vegetables. Coating the ladder with wood preservative will prolong its life.

At Sissinghurst, an ancient stone well-head is circled with rosy bricks and set within a manicured lawn to create a unique raised bed. The silvery tones of artemisia enhance the weathered gray tones of the venerable stone.

Hanging Planters

Hanging baskets, pots, bowls, boxes, wall troughs, hayracks, and mangers help gardeners add height to the garden, drawing the eye, and sometimes the nose, upward. A group of skillfully planted and placed hanging containers will block an unattractive view from a window, terrace, deck, or balcony while adding color, scent, and texture to the site.

Hanging containers are most often made of wood, terra-cotta, plastic, wire mesh, or plastic-coated wire. Some have simple wire arms with a hook for hanging. More elaborate, and actually more attractive, hanging devices are made from rope, chains, and wrought-iron rods. Hanging plant containers can be suspended from decorative hooks or from metal or wooden supports attached to walls, fences, pergolas, beams, roof overhangs, or porch supports, bringing the garden to places that might otherwise be bare.

Terra-cotta half-round pots, lead lavabos, wire plant mangers, and hayracks with one flat side, when amply planted with impatiens, begonias, ivy, fuchsias, ferns, orchids, browallia, or camellias, will fill a blank, shaded wall or fence with color. A sunnier spot will welcome ivy geraniums, coreopsis, petunias, nasturtiums, flowering kale, trailing lantana, or portulaca tucked into wall-hanging containers.

Wrought-iron shepherd's crooks, some with as many as four curved arms, make free-standing supports for hanging baskets, which can be placed anywhere in the garden, adding structural interest as well as color and scent. Simple white plastic baskets of ivy geraniums, marguerites, impatiens, petunias, sweet alyssum, torenia, or verbena direct from the garden center add instant color to a dull spot when you hang a few from a shepherd's crook. Or you might create your own hanging baskets using cuttings of favorite plants, annuals grown from seed, or houseplants brought outside for the summer. (In winter, hang bird feeders from the crooks and move them to a spot near a window so you can watch your feathered visitors.)

Remember that hanging containers are most often seen from below, making it important to pay attention to the looks of the underside when planning a planting scheme. Wire and mesh baskets look best when the plastic lining is covered up with sheet or sphagnum moss.

TOP: *Old-fashioned pansies in shades of purple, mauve, and white with purple centers suit an aged terra-cotta wall-hung pot.*

CENTER: *The soft white of a shell-shaped wall pocket supported by a chubby cherub is perfectly matched with the clear white of spring primroses. The dark green leaves of the primrose make a nice contrast.*

BOTTOM: *Ruffly mauve flowering kale, late-blooming heather, and ivy in a hanging basket add color to a winter garden. Cold weather brings out the color in the kale, which is really a dressed-up cabbage.*

Two hanging baskets overflow with cascading blooms.

ABOVE: *Ivy geraniums like this pink variety will obscure their containers in a matter of weeks when provided with plenty of sun, water, and fertilizer.*

LEFT: *Verbena 'Homestead Purple' in a moss-lined wire basket is one of the most reliable long-blooming plants.*

❧ Out-of-the-Ordinary Containers ❧

There are no limits, including the confines of good taste, to the containers gardeners use to house their plants. Who hasn't seen a floral display in a truck tire that's been turned inside out, edges cut into points and painted white? Even toilets potted up with petunias have decorated a front yard or two.

Whimsical potted gardens are often delightful exhibits of their owners' imaginative talents and inventiveness. In sunny courtyards or picturesque villages, colorful olive oil cans or cookie tins are converted to flowerpot duty. Coffee cans, milk cartons with their tops trimmed off, even plastic yogurt cups and margarine tubs sprout tiny seedlings on many a city fire escape.

Birdbaths, rowboats, wheelbarrows, cast-iron hibachis, and old boots have been artfully reincarnated when their creative owners have filled them with succulents, herbs, bright annuals, or decorative peppers.

Clay pipes, normally put to work in drainage ditches, become flowerpots when cut into one-foot (30cm) sections, up-ended, and filled with soil. Chimney pots, some with decorative edging, have been pressed into flower duty too, adding a little vertical interest to their surroundings.

A toy dump truck, an enameled coffeepot, and a vintage mailbox have all been transformed when a little soil and a few plants are tucked inside. A

cut-glass goblet, a Depression-era glass ice bucket, and a slightly chipped chamber pot all make fine containers for forcing bulbs when filled with marbles or gravel to support the roots.

Nearly any found object, as long as it sports a hollow space, will serve as a place to pot up a plant. Some, like a reed basket or a bird's nest, won't last many seasons. Sturdier containers—an old cracked butter crock or a big conch shell, for instance—might last for generations.

TOP: An imaginative gardener has tucked a sunny primrose into the hollowed cavity of a dried gourd, which sits on an upturned pot-cum-pedestal.

BOTTOM: An empty spot of earth in the garden is whimsically fitted with a pair of cement shoes where a clump of chives and a family of hens-and-chicks are comfortably at home.

OPPOSITE: Past its usefulness as a garden workhorse, a creaky old wheelbarrow spends its retirement as an oversized container for a riotous collection of blooms. Unless lined with plastic or treated with rust-proofing paint, the wheelbarrow will eventually corrode from the effects of water. But while it lasts, it serves as a wonderful container.

A pair of wellies tucked into a doorway corner sprouts rich red begonias, artemisia, and variegated ivy.

Winter Care of Terra-cotta Pots

Because of their porous nature and their relative fragility, terra-cotta pots and planters will often crack, flake, or shatter when exposed to frost or freezing conditions. If your pots survive the first winter, pressure from soil and roots which have absorbed moisture is likely to crack the pots by the second year of exposure. So, though some gardeners have had success leaving terra-cotta containers out all winter when they rest on a bed of stones rather than a paved surface, it's most often best to bring them indoors in winter if you can.

Before putting terra-cotta pots away, though, it's a good idea to prepare them for storage so they'll be in good shape for use in the spring.

First, remove plant material and soil (put it on the compost pile if no diseases or pests are present). Brush off any clinging soil or roots with a stiff brush or rag.

Remove mineral and dirt residues by soaking the pots in a big tub in a mixture of vinegar and water (about one cup [250ml] of vinegar to one gallon [3.8L] of water) for a few hours. Allow them to dry thoroughly, then store in the garage, toolshed, basement, or greenhouse away from water and frost.

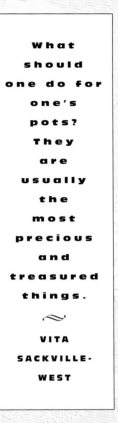

What should one do for one's pots? They are usually the most precious and treasured things.

—VITA SACKVILLE-WEST

Plastic Pots

The many uses of plastic pots in the potted garden should not be overlooked. Plastic's lightweight nature makes it useful for rooftop or balcony gardens, and for holding large tender plants which must be moved indoors in winter. The elderly or disabled, for whom lifting may be difficult, may prefer to plant their potted gardens in plastic containers because they are easier to move about than those made of other materials.

Plastic trays and pots are excellent containers in which to grow annuals from seed before transplanting to their summer habitats. Plastic planters are durable, as they won't chip, decompose, or break when dropped. And plastic pots, because they are not porous, will enable the soil to retain moisture, thus requiring less frequent watering.

However, even the best plastic pots, though they are made to look very much like terra-cotta, are just not as aesthetically pleasing as the pots they are intended to imitate. Gardeners might benefit from all the advantages of plastic, but keep the pots hidden with foliage from another plant, or by placing them inside other, more decorative pots which then serve as cachepots.

TYPES OF

From rooftop to basement entrance, venues

for potted gardens abound. City properties

with nary a blade of grass and majestic country

estates have wildly different needs, yet each

is a likely home for a potted garden.

*Pots in gardens sometimes make more of a visual statement
when they are left empty. The simple lines of this glazed urn
lighten a dark brick corner. Framing the urn is a
thick growth of variegated nasturtiums that have totally
masked the simple pots in which they are growing.*

POTTED GARDENS

～ Entrance Gardens ～

The most public aspect of your home, the entrance, offers visitors the first glimpse of your personality, tastes, and style. What better spot to place a few exquisite plants in ornamental pots?

City and town houses, unlike their suburban and country cousins, are often separated from the street or sidewalk by inhospitable and unattractive paving and harsh, barren vertical space. How much more attractive these urban scenes become when the occupant adorns the entrance with potted plants!

Variegated hostas in shades of green and cream make a bold, decorative statement, adding a stippled, light effect when massed in pots in a dark entrance corner. Liriope, or turf lily, varieties will do well here, too, with the bonus of spiky pink or violet flowers and dark wands of fruit.

Good groupings of smaller plants in pots is a form of ornament that might be made more use of in our gardens, especially where there are paved spaces near a house.

～

GERTRUDE JEKYLL, *COLOR SCHEMES FOR THE FLOWER GARDEN*

Large tubs on either side of a sunny entranceway might hold climbing roses that clamber up the walls joining hands across the top of the door and creating an island of cottage ambiance in a cityscape. Select an everblooming or repeat-blooming variety, such as 'Golden Rambler' (which is also known as 'Alister Stella Gray'), 'Allen Chandler', 'Blush Noisette', 'Belle de Londres', or 'Iceberg', to ensure abundant color.

Any number of vines grown in large planters or permanent raised beds can be trained to climb the walls surrounding an entrance. Wisteria in shades of purple or stark white will eventually cover an entire building if given half a chance. Militant pruning will not only keep this rampant climber within bounds, but will also encourage a wealth of highly perfumed blooms. Tough ivies, planted in pots and trained up the wall, will

The screen-door entrance to an unpretentious shingle cottage is graciously flanked by a pair of planted vignettes. Placed on a terraced "stage," the imaginative planting includes neatly clipped topiaries, ivies, geraniums, salvia and heliotrope.

A pair of ornate cement pots holds bright yellow primroses in early spring outside a brick and tile entrance in Kent. Later in the season, the owners may add pansies, geraniums, tuberous begonias, or other colorful seasonal blooms.

quickly surround a doorway with a green frame. Ivy will not damage mortar that is in good repair. It will actually protect brick walls because it keeps rain off and insulates against freeze-thaw damage. Ivy will, however, damage stucco and plaster walls and should be avoided in those situations.

You might wish to acknowledge the march of the seasons with a changing display of potted plants flanking a doorway, commencing with daffodils or tulips in the spring and progressing through the summer months with an unfolding pageant of peonies, iris, lilies, campanulas, hydrangea, and veronicas, followed in fall by daisies, asters, and mums. In harsh winter zones, miniature evergreen trees, bedecked with tiny white lights and little red bows, mark the holiday season before the cycle starts again. It helps to have "offstage" storage for those potted plants waiting for their cue.

For anyone planning an entrance garden in the city, it is important to ensure that plants will get enough light and that they will not be choked by automobile exhaust or other forms of air pollution. Another important consideration is some people's unfortunate habit of taking what doesn't belong to them. Large, valuable containers will need to be secured by affixing them permanently into the paving or by running a chain through the drainage hole and linking it to an immovable object.

In a more countrified setting, a collection of potted dahlias marching up the steps of a front porch greets the postman with the same cheerful enthusiasm as it does dinner guests. A hay rack, packed with a mix of colorful annuals and attached to a wall next to the front door, lends a casual ornamental touch.

A front porch furnished with a set of vintage wicker will look completely dressed when the wicker plant stand is brimming with lush ferns, vibrant primroses, velvety pansies, or cool impatiens.

OPPOSITE: *An especially lovely composition of Skimmia japonica, coral bells, pansies, and variegated ivy shows the hand of a skilled designer. The tile terrace, terra-cotta pot and like-colored brick wall would dissolve into a uninteresting blur with a lesser combination of plants.*

LEFT: *The grand arched entry court at Sissinghurst is guarded on either side by old terra-cotta pots holding a mass of simple purple pansies. The purple of the pansies intensifies the colors of the climbing roses.*

⤳ Terrace Gardens ⤺

The terrace, patio, courtyard, palazzo, or whatever you call that paved part of your property just outside the back or side door, may serve as a transitional space to the garden or, for city and town dwellers, may in fact be all the garden you have. Some people refer to rooftop gardens as terraces, but here, we'll use the word "terrace" to mean a ground-level space.

Whether small and intimate or spacious and open, the terrace is an ideal location for a potted garden. Plants in containers can define spaces; produce angles or curves where none existed; add color, scent, and texture; create a sense of mystery and surprise; become a focal point; and, of course, provide boundless beauty.

A series of garden rooms, reminiscent of a small-scale Hidcote or Sissinghurst, is fashioned on a long, narrow terrace by the adroit positioning of leafy plants in large containers. Seating or dining areas are defined by groupings of small potted trees or large shrubs in tubs. Evergreen trees planted in deep, raised-perimeter beds will effectively hide unpleasant urban views from a backyard terrace. And a utility area can be screened from sight when a long, narrow planter is topped with a trellis hung with lush vines.

A formal atmosphere can be created on a brick terrace when straight rows of neatly clipped potted boxwood form a square with a standard rose in a caisse Versailles at each corner. By contrast, a sense of the countryside is evoked on a city terrace when an eclectic collection of tubs and pots is filled with daisies, geraniums, heliotropes, petunias, and other unpretentious annuals.

A sense of mystery and surprise, one of the most difficult elements to introduce to a garden, can be achieved on a terrace by creating a curving path outlined with densely planted pots. Be sure to place a focal point at the end of the path—perhaps a gorgeous fuchsia in an especially beautiful cast-iron urn atop a stone plinth or a spectacular cut-leaf Japanese maple in an ornamental terra-cotta pot.

A terrace is also the perfect site for a fountain or pool. Surround a formal two-tiered cast-iron fountain with a gathering of tall white tulips, clipped box, rosemary topiaries, dwarf conifers, blue-green hostas, or 'Stella d'Oro' daylilies in matching pots. Or assemble a countrified display of ferns, verbena, lady's mantle, impatiens, browallia, and daisies.

OPPOSITE, TOP: *This intimate paved courtyard in Surrey is lush with plants including towering 'Casa Blanca' lilies, fuschias, and geraniums in hanging baskets, silvery artemisia, and simple white petunias and sedum in a central urn.*

OPPOSITE, BOTTOM: *Checkerboard brick paving and wrought-iron gates strike a formal pose on this terrace, but the robust terra-cotta pots overflowing with down-to-earth red and white geraniums make for a more relaxed scene.*

TOP, LEFT: *Vase-shaped rhubarb pots punctuate the York stone paving of a garden terrace. Repetition of shape helps pull an eclectic group of components— rectangular stones, gravel, garden swings, and a profusion of plantings—into a cohesive design.*

BOTTOM, LEFT: *A pair of bistro chairs frames a collection of potted plants on a wood deck. Plenty of plants in containers will help to define or enclose more intimate spaces on an open deck or terrace.*

Masses of bright red geraniums in terra-cotta pots emphasize the warm adobe colors of this Santa Fe terrace. The same courtyard could also happily accommodate rustic wooden containers of sunflowers, portulaca, and gaillardia; bougainvillea in hanging baskets; or large containers with red, orange, and yellow hibiscus or decorative native grasses.

⮌ Rooftop and Balcony Gardens ⮌

Raised perimeter beds backed by tall trellis "walls" provide privacy without restricting light or air circulation in this rooftop garden. Vertical interest has been added with tall shrubs, climbing roses, and vines. Evergreen shrubs and clumps of groundcovers fill the planters while seasonal plants spill over the sides, softening the linear shapes.

Looking out the window of a high-rise building, one is amazed at the pockets of privacy and the occasional oases of green that city gardeners have ingeniously created for themselves within the confines of a rooftop or a balcony.

The physical properties of rooftop and balcony gardens present a set of concerns that don't exist in other gardens. Of greatest importance is the weight-bearing structural abilities of the roof or balcony. The gardener must determine how much weight the roof can support, and where the structural supports are located, for the heaviest containers—permanent planters and large tubs and pots—will need to be located directly above the weight-bearing supports.

One must also think about water—not only where a convenient source of water will be, but also what will happen to the water that drains through the planters. The roof itself must be totally waterproof before any garden additions are made, and arrangements must be made to allow excess water to drain off the roof.

This can become a complicated and difficult affair. Think about hauling wood, piping, soil, gravel, and plants up to a rooftop!

Once the structural aspects of a rooftop or balcony garden are accounted for, however, the more pleasant task of selecting plants and containers can be approached. And, here again, these gardens differ from their earthbound relatives. The higher

the building, the stronger destructive, moisture-robbing winds will be. Care must be taken to choose plants that can stand up to these difficult conditions.

If your rooftop or balcony garden cannot support the weight of permanent planters in which to plant a living windbreak of arborvitae, junipers, or Japanese pine, you might consider constructing a lattice fence on which to train ivy, grape, wisteria, trumpet vine, or Virginia creeper to grow from a planter at its feet.

Place small shrubs—dwarf rhododendrons and azaleas, *Pieris*, *Chamaecyparis*, Scotch broom, hydrangea, euonymous, daphne, or viburnum—in containers up against the trellis or close to walls where they have some protection.

A long, narrow rooftop garden might be divided into "rooms," much the way a terrace is, with the judicious placement of large planters and tall plants.

Small trees like weeping cherry, birch, crab apple, or Russian olive planted against the southern and western skies will provide shady spots.

Even the poshest penthouse garden has limited space, so use every square inch. Under-plant trees and shrubs with perennial foliage including hosta, liriope, ferns, and low-growing ornamental grasses.

Design a succession of blooms with perennials in smaller pots. Tuck spring- and fall-flowering bulbs in amongst ground covers. Espalier small trees against walls, fences, and railings. Make use of hanging planters. Encourage vines to grow.

ABOVE LEFT: *The relatively monochromatic black and white theme of this contemporary deck with climbing roses is punctuated by simple combinations of brightly colored geraniums, lobelia, and New Guinea impatiens in terra-cotta pots. Note the saucers under the pots—essential to preventing water from accumulating on wooden deck flooring.*

ABOVE RIGHT: *This urban rooftop garden is colorfully and eclectically planted with canna lilies, impatiens, geraniums, and trailing ivy. The new wooden arbor is strong enough to support heavy vines, which will eventually provide the terrace with cooling shade.*

Wind-resistant Plants

Most plants aren't happy in strong winds. Wind will stress plants by whipping their leaves and branches, and will cause them to dry out quickly. But some plants will tolerate more wind than others.

Junipers (especially *Juniperus virginiana* 'Skyrocket'), yews, arborvitae, Japanese black pine, and holly are evergreen shrubs that will withstand the strong winds that lash across a rooftop and will form a windscreen to protect other plants. Birch, sea buckthorn, crab apples, mahonia, barberry, bayberry, and Russian olive are good choices where winds are a problem, as are yuccas and some roses, most notably *Rosa rugosa*.

Also suitable for exposed sites are broom, santolinas, sedum, ivy, Virginia creeper, and heaths and heathers.

⤳ Water Gardens ⤳

Even the smallest garden will have space for a pool or pond. And who wouldn't want to have one? Water in the garden adds an element of delight and playfulness. It has the ability to evoke a feeling of peaceful serenity. With the addition of a bubbler, a small jet, or fountain, the water garden brings relaxing sound and mesmerizing movement into the picture.

You can create a water garden in a rustic wooden tub for a balcony garden. A good-size ceramic bowl with a pair of water lilies becomes a beckoning pool on a city rooftop. An old iron pot, lush with cattails, a few grasses,

Water gardens are planted in what amount to sunken containers. The Siberian iris and Iris pseudacorus *are held in pots that rest just below the surface of this water garden. Japanese iris will also grow under these conditions.*

I like to see clear water in the middle, reflecting the sky and the plants which you will have set round the edge.

⤳

VITA SACKVILLE-WEST ON POOL GARDENS

and water-loving iris, is the ideal water element for a sunny corner of the terrace or rooftop.

With interest in water gardens growing, many companies now manufacture containers designed for above- or below-ground placement. Aquatic plants are sold through mail-order catalogs, and there are many books devoted exclusively to the subject of water gardening.

Water gardens in prefabricated concrete pools, faux granite containers, or large ceramic bowls will have a formal flavor when centered in a paved area or lawn. A flat surface surrounding the pool, whether it is

Water Plants

Some gardeners devote all their time to the intricacies of aquatic plants. But with just a little effort, even a novice gardener will enjoy success with some of the water plants listed here.

Plants for water gardens are divided into two basic categories—aquatics, those plants that actually have their roots in the soil at the bottom of the pool; and marginals, which grow in water, but are most often planted in pots which are then placed in the pool, sometimes on ledges or stands so they aren't totally submerged.

+ Waterlilies (*Nymphaea*). Most of the dozens of water lilies commercially available are tender, but *Nymphaea* 'Chromatella' is a hardy variety. It produces 3-inch (7.5cm) pale yellow flowers with darker yellow centers on classic lily pads. *Nymphaea* 'Tina' is a gorgeous purple waterlily with yellow centers and is especially appropriate for a small tank or tub.

+ Cattail (*Typha*). A dwarf variety, 'Minima', is just the right size for a whiskey barrel water garden. It has round, brown flowers above spiky foliage.

+ Parrot's feather (*Myriophyllum aquaticum*). This plant's feathery curling stems float on the water's surface.

+ Arrowhead (*Sagittaria montevidensis*). As the name suggests, this plant's leaves resemble arrows. It has white flowers with a dot of purple at the base.

+ Water forget-me-not (*Myosotis scorpioides*). Light blue flowers with yellow eyes above low-lying foliage.

+ Water violet (*Hottonia palustris*). Spikes of purple or white flowers. The feathery foliage stays underwater, where it works as an oxygenator.

For books with extensive listings of aquatic plants, see suggested reading (page118).

submerged or above ground, will enhance the formal styling of such a pool.

Free-form water gardens made with prefabricated plastic liners or forms that are placed in excavations in the garden make naturalistic ponds where lush plantings of aquatic and bog area plants will thrive, and where frogs and perhaps fish will find a comfortable home.

While water gardening is essentially uncomplicated, there are a few rules to follow in order to keep water conditions suitable. The container should be at least one foot (30cm) deep, and of course it must be watertight. Try to include a plant with oxygenating qualities like pondweed, willow moss, starwort, or *Myriophyllum*. Include a floating plant like water lily or water hyacinth and some grasses or rushes for an interesting mix of colors, textures, and sizes.

It's important to remember that most aquatic plants prefer a sunny location, that falling leaves from nearby trees will foul your water garden and kill the plants, and that water gardens don't prosper in windy areas.

Nymphae (water lily) is a genus of deciduous, summer-flowering plants that float on the surface of the water with their rhizomes growing in soil on the pond bottom. While some, like 'Attraction', with deep red flowers, or 'American Star', a pink, are completely hardy to Zone 5, others, like 'Emily Grant Hutchings', a pink, or 'Margaret Mary', a blue variety, are only happy in Zones 9 or 10. Gardeners in colder climates frequently grow the tender varieties as annuals.

A massive terra-cotta pot lush with roses adorns a corner of a large stone-edged pond. Iris and water lilies are equally at home here. The simplicity of the pot and the roses strikes just the right tone when combined with the chartreuse and purple of surrounding plantings.

∽ Accents in the Garden ∽

RIGHT: *There are times when an empty container is needed to make a design complete. A large sculpted urn is a focal point in the center of a box- and rose-edged square. From certain vantage points, the urn seems to be framed by the pointed arch of a doorway guarded by a pair of tall citrus trees.*

BELOW: *Without a row of mossy osteospermum-filled terra-cotta pots placed at regular intervals, this railroad tie and gravel flight of steps might not make the strong visual statement it does.*

Have you ever visited a garden where, despite the fact that the plants were beautiful, there was no memorable sight to take away with you? It may have been because the garden lacked a focal point or important accents that engaged your eye, drawing you into the garden and making the whole scheme work.

Plants in pots are often expertly employed to play the role of focal point or ornamental accent in tiny town gardens, on suburban decks or poolsides, or on the grounds of majestic country homes.

At Highgrove, HRH the Prince of Wales' estate in Gloucestershire, pots and planters are used extensively to make visual statements within the landscape design. A massive terra-cotta jar topped with petunias is strategically placed in the center of a honeysuckle-covered pergola in the walled garden, serving as the focal point at the end of a path.

On the stone terrace, dwarf fruit trees in terra-cotta pots and geraniums in terra-cotta jars make bold, vertical accents and balance the strong visual impact of a stone pavilion. Elsewhere, a rustic wood pergola is anchored by a pair of clipped evergreens in ornamental pots.

Encircling the spouting fountain in the courtyard of the Spanish Governor's Palace in San Antonio, Texas, are a dozen red geraniums in simple terra-cotta pots. Although they are among the most common of flowers in equally unpretentious pots, the arrangement serves to draw immediate attention to the fountain, enhancing its elegance.

At Sissinghurst, one of the world's most visited gardens, gardeners make significant use of plants in pots as accents and focal points, following the lead of the garden's originators. Outside the library is a huge lead tank adorned with a pattern of the Tudor rose. The tank is set into a niche in the wall and is filled with fuchsias. The effect is to draw the eye to a relatively obscure corner, which then becomes the stage for a delightful presentation of color and form.

In the center of the hedge-enclosed herb garden, and serving as its focal point, sits a huge Italian stone bowl supported by stone lions. Low-growing sedums make a modest understudy to the bowl's dramatic presence.

There are as many ways to make a bold accent with potted plants as there are gardeners to design them. Here are some ideas:

❧ March two rows of identical potted plants (geraniums, verbena, tulips, daffodils, boxwood, daisies, liriope, whatever) up a set of stairs to make a dramatic entrance.

❧ Punctuate a straight walkway with potted topiary rosemary or box, rose, or juniper standards.

❧ Encircle a pool, fountain, sundial, or armillary with alternating pots of round and conical clipped box.

❧ Place a gorgeous red cut-leaf maple at the end of a curving path.

❧ Stand a cast-iron urn with a mass of a single colored plant on a stone plinth in the center of intersecting paths in an herb or knot garden.

❧ Place a white wisteria standard in an enormous tub just to one side of a white cast-iron bench. Sometimes asymmetry is more dramatic than the more expected symmetry.

❧ Add contrast to a monochromatic scene (against a hedge, wall, or fence; in a grouping of foliage plants) with one big pot of flowers or foliage of a contrasting color.

❧ Fill in for faded flowers. When the daffodils and tulips have passed, put a big pot of pansies or primroses in the empty space. Do the same after the poppies, bleeding hearts, and lilies have said their good-byes. (Take care not to cover ripening leaves or they'll be unable to soak up the sun's rays, which is how the plants store nutrients to fuel next year's show.)

❧ Add temporary color to your potted garden while a newcomer becomes established. Newly planted shrubs, vines, or perennials may take a season or more to make a noticeable debut in beds and borders. Disguise their immature stages with stand-ins in the form of reliable performers in decorative pots.

Masses of annuals, in this case geraniums, lobelia, and argyranthemum, become an accent in a corner of a paved garden. The gardener has cleverly varied the sizes, shapes, and textures of the plants to create an interesting and attractive tableau.

A well-planted container becomes a dramatic focal point in the center of a paved garden space. Here, the spiky swordlike leaves of phormium echo the red, yellow, and burgundy shades in the surrounding plantings. A rose, abutilon, lantana, or hibiscus standard in a grand lead planter, a massive datura in a cast-iron urn, an exquisite Japanese maple in a weathered wooden box, or a gnarled agave in a ceramic bowl are other examples of dramatic plantings that might be used as focal points in the garden.

⌒ At Window Level ⌒

A well-filled window box is a gardener's generous gift to all who pass by. Who knows how much we will brighten another's day by sharing our colorful plants with neighbors and strangers alike?

Though we most often think of window boxes as decoration for quaint country cottages, alpine chalets, or rustic beach houses, cleverly designed window boxes adorn New York brownstones, London town houses, and Mediterranean villas with equal ease. Even stark contemporary buildings will gladly accommodate living window treatments.

Fire escapes, generally unattractive facts of life in cities, are wonderful sites for potted gardens, as long as they never interfere with emergency egress or with city safety codes.

As with all potted gardens, the key to window box success is selecting the most suitable container and the best plants to put in it.

Before this, however, the first consideration when planning a window garden is safety. You don't want to court disaster with an insecure planter perched precariously above the street. Windowsill gardens are among the few places where plastic or fiberglass containers, because of their lighter weight, are apt to be more appropriate than those made of other materials. Traditional cedar or redwood window boxes, often with a plastic liner, are also good choices. And a wire hayrack attached to a windowsill or to a wall just under the window is an attractive alternative.

There are several methods for mounting window boxes securely. At a window with a deep sill, the box will rest on the sill, fastened with bolts through the bottom or with hooks to the window frame. Where windowsills are narrow, the box is supported on brackets affixed to the wall. A wire planter can be attached with hooks.

Terra-cotta planters and cement containers are also used as window boxes, although great care must be taken to fasten them. Cement should be used only in situations with very deep, very strong stone or brick sills. Pots on a fire escape are the lone exception to the rule that all window planters must be firmly affixed. However, it's a good idea to use some kind of a shallow box or tray on which to set potted plants on the fire escape to prevent any from accidentally tumbling.

Another very important consideration for window-box gardening is the effort needed to keep

TOP: *Window boxes planted with annual flowers and morning glory vines soften the hard angles of a large window. Provided with a string or wire to climb, morning glories, moon flowers, scarlet runner beans, and other lightweight vines are useful at window level.*

BOTTOM: *The weathered green of the shutters surrounding the lace-curtained window is repeated in the various shades of green of geranium cuttings in simple terra-cotta pots. Placing potted plants just outside a window is a satisfying way to bring the pleasures of the garden into the house.*

the plants in your boxes watered. Boxes at a first-floor window are easy to reach with a long-necked watering can or a wand on the end of a hose. At higher levels, water the boxes through an open window. If this is not an easy task, reconsider having window boxes, for they will need daily watering in dry, hot weather.

Window boxes, as with any potted garden, must have plenty of drainage holes, so when you irrigate, some water will pass through. Keep in mind that passersby will not appreciate an unexpected midmorning shower!

With safety and maintenance considerations taken care of, the fun begins. Window boxes are like a noisy family picnic where a few more guests are happily accommodated, and the ambiance is as important as the menu.

For summer displays, crowd as many plants into the container as you can.

Fill a planter with masses of multicolored tuberous begonias and some variegated ivy to trail below. Or mix white petunias, pale blue browallia, pink ivy geraniums, darker pink nicotianas, purple salvia spikes, and bold purple cups of lisianthus for an exuberant, cool-color display.

If hot colors are more your style, plant trailing yellow and orange nasturtiums, miniature zinnias in reds and scarlets, calendulas, gazanias, marigolds, and portulaca for a riot of color.

Their stay will be brief, so you will want to make the most of it. Keep them well-watered and fed and they will reward you with a joyful show.

More permanent window plantings are also possible. With a deep enough box, plenty of water, and regular feeding, dwarf shrubs and trees can be successfully cultivated on windowsills. A trio of dwarf evergreen *Chamaecyparis lawsoniana* matched with an underplanting of miniature hostas and ivy makes a formal statement.

Dwarf rhododendrons and azaleas underplanted with mini daffodils, grape hyacinth, crocus, or smaller bulbs will offer springtime delight. Miniature roses and perennial herbs like lavender, thyme, or rosemary can prosper in window boxes where winters aren't harsh. In shady spots, evergreen ferns and liriope will provide greenery.

Window boxes packed with annual herbs, small vegetable plants, and strawberries, especially the tiny and delicious *fraises des bois*, will fulfill the city dweller's craving for fresh produce.

Utterly simple and unpretentious, this homemade window box planted with young red petunias announces the beginning of summer. With daily watering in dry weather, regular feeding, and scrupulous dead-heading all season, these petunias will reward the gardener with season-long bloom.

Gardens for the Disabled

Dolly Robertson tends her long, narrow suburban garden outside London, growing bushels of vegetables in terra-cotta pots and giant concrete containers. Confined to a wheelchair and limited to the use of only one hand, Dolly, who celebrated her eightieth birthday in 1995, raises onions, beans, tomatoes, strawberries, rhubarb, and more, with plenty for herself and neighbors.

Horticultural therapists, pioneers in a relatively new field, have found that the basic tasks involved in growing plants are beneficial to their clients, particularly the elderly and the disabled. For some, it evokes warm memories of a childhood spent on farms or pleasant afternoons in long-forgotten gardens. For others, the very act of planting and nurturing beautiful living things is therapeutic and healing.

Bending, lifting, even walking, are often difficult or impossible for the elderly or disabled. Raised beds connected by evenly paved garden paths, window boxes mounted on the inside railings of a deck or balcony, or a collection of containers on tabletops will prove especially suitable for those with physical disabilities.

When planning a garden for a disabled person, place raised beds or containers at an appropriate height for a comfortable stool, chair, or wheelchair. Be sure that paths are wide enough to accommodate a wheelchair and that paving surfaces are smooth. A water source should be close at hand. Raised beds or large tubs are readily adapted for use by gardeners with impaired vision, who will welcome a diversity of plants with subtle scents and a variety of textures and shapes. A system of railings and markers might be installed to assist the blind gardener in finding her way about the planting area.

Seasonal Displays

A potted garden is so versatile! With just a little effort, you can honor the change of seasons with an ongoing horticultural celebration.

Welcome the newness of spring with pots full of tulips, daffodils, crocus, or hyacinth. Primroses or pansies come a few weeks later.

Late spring through late summer, the potted garden will be bursting with the blooms of annuals and perennials, so you'll have time to sit back and enjoy it.

In the fall, fill containers with chrysanthemums—all of a color for a formal setting, or every color you can find to create a casual scene. Plant a big wooden tub with a huge clump of goldenrod and surround it with pumpkins and gourds. Introduce the pink and green frilly mounds of flowering kale to your window boxes, and move potted ornamental shrubs or small trees whose leaves have taken on their autumn colors to a spot where they will take center stage.

Dress up a terrace, balcony, or entranceway for the Christmas holidays with miniature spruce trees in formal white-painted boxes. Trim them with red or gold bows, tiny ornamental birds in little nests, or twinkling white lights.

Fill empty concrete or stone planters with branches of cut greens—pine, yew, hemlock, and holly. Add a few bunches of white-painted twigs for height and emphasis.

In areas where the holiday season is more temperate, fill a tiered wire plant stand with red and white poinsettias for a party on the terrace. Or string lights around a pair of standard bay trees to brighten up your front doorway.

Force narcissus, grape hyacinth, and amaryllis bulbs in ceramic bowls indoors to carry you through the winter months until the early bulbs begin to bloom outdoors.

Chapter 3

DESIGNING A

A quantity of plants in pots
standing in various parts
of the garden...form an important
part of the garden design.

∼

GERTRUDE JEKYLL

To create a beautiful potted garden, we need the same skills we draw upon to design foundation plantings, perennial beds, mixed borders, or suburban landscapes.

The gardener must start with a solid understanding of the physical and logistical variables of the space—where the sun shines and where it doesn't, boundaries, existing architectural and horticultural features, prevailing winds, water sources, and municipal codes.

The pots resting on a paved space between foundation and lawn in this garden are all but obscured by the abundant collection of plants they contain. While the image is one of only-slightly-controlled exuberance, the designer has cleverly combined colors, textures, and shapes to make an effective display.

POTTED GARDEN

W hen you begin to design your garden, it's essential to have in mind how it will be used—for casual family fun, elegant entertaining, a quiet retreat for reading and relaxing, a manageable garden experience for a young child, a striking focal point, or a place to indulge horticultural interests. Most gardens fulfill a combination of purposes.

The style of the potted garden will be determined by personal taste and the site's physical characteristics, as well as your budget, time, and interest. And the elements one incorporates—color, scale, style, shape, and texture—will determine the character of the finished product.

This chapter looks at some of the factors to consider when designing a potted garden.

An unusual combination of plants, including lirope, daylilies, agave, iris, and ligularia, repeats similar swordlike leaf shapes, but with different widths and textures. Colors, too, are artfully used. Note how well the burgundy red of the compact barberry, the cream and gold tones of the agave, and the gold of the daylily complement each other.

❧ Purpose ❧

What do you expect from your potted garden? Each gardener will have a different answer. A touch of green in an urban environment. Privacy on a terrace. Ornamental elements on a deck. Enhancement of an already elaborate garden plan. A reliable source of color. A gardening project for parents and children to do together. Culinary herbs just outside the kitchen door. The opportunity to work with exotic tender plants in a cold-weather climate.

The reasons are infinite and sometimes multiple. Because potted gardens are so versatile and so varied, every gardener should be able to have his or her needs and desires fulfilled.

But before starting out on any potted garden project, it is wise to sit down with a pen and paper to write out one's objectives. Just a few words or a complex design philosophy may result, but no matter what form it takes, you'll have a better understanding of what your needs and expectations are. Be sure to refer to your list from time to time. Your ideas and plans may change along the way, but you won't lose sight of your goals.

ABOVE: *Though seemingly effortless, combining diverse elements, such as this weathered wooden chair, pebble mosaic paving, and a clipped topiary in a simple pot, especially in a small space, takes a good eye, imagination, and a willingness to experiment. Working with plants in pots makes it easy, however, to try a variety of plants and placements.*

LEFT: *High-maintenance potted plants would be out of place in a low-maintenance cactus garden. Instead, reliable, easy-to-please geraniums are ideal for providing color and a rounded shape amid the thorny green spikes of the cacti.*

⟶ Style ⟶

Just as when we decorate and furnish our homes, we embrace a style for our gardens. Formal or relaxed. Rustic or urban. Extravagant or conservative. Lively or serene. Colorful or monochromatic. Focused or eclectic. A sense of style is personal, often innate, but we can adopt the ideas others have perfected, then adapt them using our own inspirations and creativity.

A potted garden should complement the style of the dwelling. A brick town house with a paved terrace, for example, will be well served by a formal, repetitive grouping of plants in pots, perhaps surrounding a fountain or a knot garden in a raised bed. A more casual approach will be achieved by grouping plants of varying sizes and shapes in an army of unmatched pots.

A sun-baked stone pool terrace will take its style cues from the surrounding arid landscape. Here low stone and terra-cotta bowls of sedums, succulents, and cacti along with large wooden tubs filled with Mexican sage, agave, and ornamental grasses make a dramatic, and appropriate, statement.

At the seashore, a contemporary home with elaborate multilevel decks demands a spare, sleek styling of its plants in pots. A single, massive cast-stone planter featuring a perfect Japanese pine, hydrangea, palm, or yucca will stand up to the most discriminating eye.

A Victorian house with gingerbread adorning its wraparound front porch will present potted plants in a totally different style. Instead of sleek or dramatic, the planters will be detailed and fancy—a frilly wire plant stand or wicker planter lush with ferns standing in a corner while a pair of cast-iron urns with regal agapanthus, spiky cordyline, or showy lantana flanks the entrance.

The garden surrounding a tiny stone cottage could hold an assortment of beloved pots collected over the years, each one thoughtfully planted every year with favorite annuals.

The gracious wicker-furnished porch of a Victorian house would not be completely dressed without a few plants in pots. Cool pink impatiens and bright tuberous begonias thrive on the shaded porch.

∽ Color ∾

Color is largely a personal issue. For the same reasons we might have an abundance of blue sweaters or red ties in our closets, or why the sight of yellow wallpaper makes us cringe, we have very personal reactions to color in the garden.

Our tastes in color have to do with our visual perceptions (the individual way we see things), our memories and upbringings, and our level of comfort with change, disharmony, and contrasts.

So, there are no truly right or wrong colors for a potted garden. That does not mean, however, that we should ignore certain color "rules."

In the scientific sense, color is the visible spectrum of light. We see color in varying hues (red, orange, yellow, green, blue, and violet), values (the lightness or darkness of the color), intensity (dullness or brightness). There are also tones, tints, and shades of colors.

To create harmony with color, artists pair colors that are next to each other on the color wheel, a graphic illustration of color that looks like a pie chart, with each triangular section representing a different color. One of the easiest to understand is based on primary colors (red, blue, and yellow) and secondary hues (orange, green, and violet). Red is between orange and violet. Yellow is between orange and green. Blue is between green and violet. Complementary colors, such as red and green, are diametrically opposed to each other; harmonizing colors, such as yellow and orange, are adjacent; contrasting colors, such as orange and violet, do not touch except at the center of the pie. So red with orange is harmonious (because orange contains red) and similarly orange with yellow (because orange has yellow in it).

Contrasting colors, on the other hand, are those that share no pigments, such as yellow with red, yellow with blue, or blue with red. In the garden,

> *Any experienced colorist knows that the blues will be more telling— more purely blue— by the juxtaposition of rightly placed complementary color.*
>
> ∽
>
> **GERTRUDE JEKYLL**

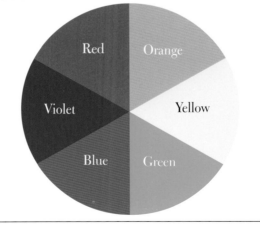

TOP: Sweet William, an easy-to-grow biennial Dianthus, *is often grown as a mix because its shades of pink, red, and white make such a lovely, lively combination, without the addition of other plants.*

CENTER: The pale green of the Echevera secunda *rosettes makes an eye-pleasing transition between the darker green of the background ivy and the cool white of the stone urn.*

BOTTOM: Just as color wheels can help designers create beautiful rooms, they can aid gardeners in creating pleasing tableaux.

contrast is also achieved by pairing dark and light colors, like pale pink and dark pink.

The many green shades provided by foliage, along with the silver and gray plants, often beautiful in their own right, provide visual transitions between contrasting colors in a garden. Adding white to a group of contrasting colors will intensify the contrast, but a grouping of white plants, combined with a range of grays, silver, and green gives a soft, restful visual affect.

Simple plants in pots—tulips, narcissi, pansies, and violas—create a sophisticated vignette with the repetition of color and form. Warm yellows complement the purple tones found in the violas and in the centers of the pansies. Pale, nearly white, narcissi ease the transition from the purple and yellow combinations to the yellow and subtle touch of red of the tulips.

White gardens have an evocative and ethereal beauty that can be achieved within the confines of a container. A terra-cotta pot becomes a contained white garden with marguerites, helichrysum, and ivy geraniums. Other choices for a similar effect could include white varieties of nicotiana, impatiens, petunias, artemisia, pansies, asters, variegated ivy, liriope, and hosta, Lychnis coronaria, lunaria, Nigeria, anemones, veronica, and stocks.

Because potted plants are often confined in smaller spaces than those in a bed or the landscape, color errors are more jarring. By taking into account how color works, you can use it successfully to brighten a dull corner, tone down a group of lusty annuals, create a focal point, and add depth to a space or make it seem more shallow. Effective use of color makes a garden "hot" or "cool," romantic, festive, formal, or casual.

Pink and mauve gardens are among the most traditional, perhaps because the combination is calming, restful, and easy on the eye. A potted garden with a long season of pink and mauve blooms might include dwarf varieties of daphne and viburnum, tulips, pink daffodils, bleeding heart, aliums, thrift, perennial cranesbill geraniums, roses, old fashioned geraniums, fuchsias, petunias, asters, hydrangea, bougainvillea, impatiens, begonias, and verbena.

A "hot" garden uses sulphur yellows, oranges, and reds to make a bold, vibrant, eye-catching statement. These strong colors will make a space seem smaller and shallower, so use them with care in a confined spot. Because hot colors draw the eye immediately, they are useful to define a focal point or to draw the

eye to a distant area. Hot colors in a window box or a hanging basket, for example, will get more attention than their paler, less demanding relatives.

Good candidates for potted plants in the hot family include yellow, orange, and red varieties of tulips, daffodils (not the pale varieties), crocus, pansies, coreopsis, dahlias, lilies, euphorbia, roses, California poppies, calendula (also called pot marigold), marigolds, geraniums, and sunflowers.

Blue gardens are rich and rewarding, often calm, restful places, and always romantic. Pots of blue plants, including those in the violet and lavender range, will expand the visual depth of a space, making it seem larger and more open than it actually is. A successful blue garden might contain violets, crocus, grape hyacinth, iris, clematis, wisteria, Himalayan poppies, pansies and violas, forget-me-nots, morning glory, rosemary, catmint, campanulas, veronicas, nigella, lobelia, lavender, salvias, agapanthus, ageratum, plumbago, asters, hydrangea, Russian sage, and fescue grass.

There are innumerable color devices available to the gardener:

- Use the repetition of color, for example, a row of potted pink tulips, especially against a solid background like a box hedge or a brick wall, to create a formal mood.

- Lighten shady spaces using chartreuse colors from lady's mantle, euphorbias and euonymus, and plants with variegated leaves like hostas, yucca, Japanese sweet flag, Japanese sedge, vinca, lamium, ribbon grass, sage, thyme, and flowering maple. Variegated leaves will make the shadows seem to move the way sunlight does when it's filtered through a tree canopy.

- Use white flowers on a terrace or deck where you spend evening hours. The plants will seem to glow in the dark.

- Create harmony in your potted garden by grouping several shades of the same color.

- Add a touch of pure yellow to a dark blue scheme for a strong contrast.

- Don't overlook the contribution of colored bark, berries, twigs, and evergreen leaves in the winter garden.

Selecting color for the potted garden is not restricted to flower and foliage. The color of the container itself is part of the equation. Hot colors, for example, don't always work well with terra-cotta, unless it is a well-weathered mossy green.

⁓ Scale ⁓

Keeping to the right scale is one of the trickiest rules in garden design. And the smaller the garden, the more difficult it is to do, because mistakes are somehow magnified in a confined space.

> It's very important to keep everything to the right scale.
>
> ⁓
>
> **VITA SACKVILLE-WEST**

Scale refers to balance, proportion, and size. It does not mean that a small space must have small pots. On the contrary, there are times when one huge, oversize planter in a tiny courtyard makes perfect design sense. However, a large garden is rarely well served by an assortment of dinky little pots scattered here and there.

The success of the relationship between pot and plant is often affected by the scale of each. For example, a rose standard will look silly in a shallow bowl. Its tall trunk and top-heavy form need to be balanced by a container with some substance. A big tub or box, roughly one quarter the height of the entire planting, would be more appropriate.

An exuberant, bushy plant—hydrangea, a big clump of daisies, or lavatara, for example—will require the planter to serve as a visual anchor. It cannot appear to be lighter and less substantial than the plant it holds.

Low-growing plants almost always look best in containers that echo their shape. A tall jar planted with creeping thyme, portulaca, *Campanula garganica*, or low-growing pansies may look unbalanced, whereas a wide bowl or trough would add a pleasing equilibrium to the scene. The same tall jar, planted with the same plants, might be successful when some of the plants spill over the sides, and the height of the container can be minimized by placing several other containers of differing heights in front of it and beside it.

There are few hard and fast design rules. But one that seems to hold true is that using odd numbers of plants or containers is an effective way to achieve an attractive visual effect. A single planter standing alone will work. Three planters of varying sizes make an interesting cluster. However, two unmatched planters standing together will most often look out of sorts. Once the total number exceeds five, however, the rule no longer applies.

ABOVE: *The shallow bowl is in perfect scale with its inhabitants. Resting it on a column or plinth gives height to a display of low-growing and sprawling plants.*

CENTER: *All-of-a-kind petunias top a wide ceramic jar in a sunny country garden. A taller jar might require trailing plants to keep the plants and containers within the same scale.*

BOTTOM: *Pairs of boxwood, rounded clumps, and tall topiaries are beautifully balanced on either side of a stone entrance. The heavier, low-growing clumps anchor the group while a dark green jasmine vine tops the doorway, lending a comforting equilibrium to the scene.*

✍ Texture ✍

The spiny cacti and succulent sedum and saxifraga are not especially inviting to the touch, but their collective textures add piquant visual interest.

Texture in the garden is capable of evoking a strong response, although often we do not even realize it. Consider the velvet fabric of lamb's ears and pansies or the feathery feel of artemisia and dill. Boxwood is crisp. Poppies feel like paper. Cacti are prickly. The leaves of portulaca and sedums are succulent. Oxalis leaves are smooth and suedelike. And hostas have an odd quilted surface.

We use the sense of touch to perceive texture, but we see it, too. By combining plants of varying textures, the gardener can introduce visual as well as tactile interest.

Layering plants with different textures adds depth to a garden space. Positioning plants with distinctly dissimilar textures in close proximity makes an exciting contrast both tactilely and visually. Try an association of waxy smooth calla lilies and fluffy astilbe; or stiffly ridged hosta with the lighter, feathery leaves of rue; or perhaps the strange, spongy heads of euphorbia with airy fennel fronds.

ABOVE LEFT: *Velvety lamb's ears are exquisitely soft both to the eye and in the hand, making them a valued addition to any number of potted garden combinations.*

LEFT: *Oriental poppies, though appearing for only a brief moment, bring with them a subtle, paper-like crispness.*

ᘐ Shape ᘐ

As children, we learn how to match shapes —squares go with squares, a group of triangles goes all in a row. When we look at shape for the potted garden, however, it's in the context of design. Shape is an essential design feature, and when masterfully manipulated, will add significantly to the overall beauty of the garden.

When we consider the shapes of plants, we are actually talking about the form they take. Junipers, for example, naturally take a variety of forms—erect, conical or columnar, spreading or prostrate, rounded or compact. Boxwood, another valuable evergreen for the potted garden, is often clipped into rounded, oval, spiral, and corkscrew or conical shapes.

Daisies, an essential plant in a cottage-style garden, can be trained into a tall standard with a huge, rounded head, or left to grow in a more nat-

ural bushy clump. And apple trees can be found in erect or weeping forms, or even espaliered into a contorted shape against a wall.

Plants and their parts are spiky, serrated, fringed, bell-shaped, heart-shaped, star-shaped, elongated, attenuated, drooping, curved, straight, and flat. The variety of shapes is nearly limitless.

The challenge, then, is to use these marvelous shapes in new, exciting, compatible, attractive, harmonious, artistic, and interesting ways.

Not to be left out of any discussion of shape in the potted garden are the pots themselves. As we've seen on previous pages, pots for plants are designed in an astounding array of shapes.

In a rectangular window box, a design scheme might call for a combination of upright and cascading shapes. The shape of a wide-mouthed,

Flat yellow flower heads of dill float among feathery leaves. A tall annual herb, dill can reach three or four feet (0.9 to 1.2m) and is useful for adding height and a graceful effect to a garden, especially at the rear of a group of potted plants.

shallow container is nicely complemented by low-growing mounds of hens-and-chicks, pansies, or thyme, or the rounded form of mugo pine, little leaf box, or eastern white cedar. And an overblown angel's trumpet calls attention to the graceful lines of a classic cast-iron urn.

Here are some ways to incorporate shape into your potted garden:

- To create contrast, pair a spiky plant with swordlike foliage—cordyline, yucca, agave, palm, or liriope—with full, rounded forms from pots of hosta, verbena, hydrangea, impatiens, or lady's mantle.

- Design a hilly topography within the confines of a stone trough with a dwarf conical juniper, mounds of thrift, the draping form of *Campanula garganica*, tufts of rock jasmine, and arching alpine flax.

- Use a repetition of highly stylized shapes—pruned plants, topiaries, and standards—to

Where neatness counts, a tidy collection of organized shapes—rounded ornamental cabbages, a neatly trimmed boxwood, and a small, round pot—accent a curve in a flower-studded lawn. The slightly-out-of-control root beer–colored iris preclude the tableau from seeming contrived.

create a formal appearance. Achieve the opposite effect with a grouping of the same plant in its natural shape. A perfect example is lantana. A pair of lantana standards flanking terrace steps bespeaks a level of formality. The same plant in its natural, slightly bushy, rounded form is easygoing and relaxed.

- Make an artistic composition of the same plant in several shapes. For example, arrange a group of rounded, tiered, spiraled, and conical boxwood in matching planters.

- Add vertical interest to the garden with spiked flowers like foxglove, iris, delphinium, Asiatic lilies, calla lilies, or Darwin tulips.

- Make a horizontal statement using plants with prostrate or spreading habit. This category isn't limited to ground covers and creeping plants. A cut-leaf Japanese maple may be taller than some of the surrounding plants, but its beautifully formed branches reach out horizontally, drawing the viewer's eye outward rather than upward.

- Soften hard edges with feathery forms. Use Hinoki cypress, *Juniperus* 'Chinensis,' Japanese maple, ferns, artemisia, nigella, dusty miller, thread-leafed coreopsis, or astilbe.

- Create a tableau with a broad mix of shapes. For example, a simple water garden will look complete with flat, floating lily pads, some spikes of cattail, the finely cut leaves of parrot's feather, and curly-leafed *Juncus effusus* 'Spiralis'.

Inventive use of shapes has transformed this path-side garden corner into an exciting visual treat. The aged terra-cotta pot filled with bright daisies provides the visual transition from the hard edges of the wooden bench to the softer lines of the lady's mantle that spills from the border onto the gravel. Note, too, the distinct shapes of the straplike leaves of the variegated *Phormium* and the strong yellow spikes of *Kniphofia*.

Good Plant Marriages

Some plants just seem to go together more successfully than others. It's what garden designers call good plant marriages. Nearly every gardener has a combination or two to rely on year after year. Some combinations rely on color. Other attractive alliances are due to associations of textures and shapes. Here are a few that have worked for others. You may want to add them to your repertoire.

- Deep red tulips with pale blue forget-me-nots.

- Dark purple petunias and lobelia with white alyssum, pink Canterbury bells, Swan River daisies, and variegated *Euphorbia marginata*.

- Maroon cosmos (*Cosmos astrosanguineus*), pale pink nicotiana, spiky purple salvia, and bright yellow gazania.

- Giant alliums underplanted with lavender.

- Elephant-ear caladium paired with cotton lavender (*Santolina pinnata*).

- Euphorbia (*Euphorbia characias wulfenii*) with clematis or grapevines.

- Peonies and bearded iris.

- Lady's mantle and purple Siberian iris.

- Climbing hydrangea and ostrich ferns.

- White daisies and artemisia.

- Blue-green hosta, Japanese painted ferns, and pink astilbe.

- Yellow daffodils and grape hyacinths.

- Huge gunnera and spikes of yellow ligularia with ferns and hosta in a shade garden.

- White and orange chrysanthemums with goldenrod.

- Silvery lamb's ears, artemisia, lavender, and Veronica 'Crater Lake'.

- Coleus, New Guinea impatiens, and polka-dot plant.

- White and green *Miscanthus* grass with spikes of red lobelia or flat heads of *Sedum* 'Autumn Joy'.

- Azalea and ivy.

- Clematis underplanted with liriope.

- Cacti and California poppies.

OPPOSITE: *Tall tulips underplanted with the bright faces of oversized pansies form a classic plant marriage. Pots of bulbs, though in bloom for a relatively short time, make a glorious appearance on a terrace or as an accent in the garden. Tulips are often treated as annuals in the potted garden, and pulled out and tossed on the compost pile when their show is over.*

PLANTING

Some people seem to be born with a green thumb. For others, horticultural success seems to come from years of trial and error. Plants, however, are living things and, although specifics differ among species, varieties, and cultivars, their basic needs—water, sun, nutrients, oxygen—are relatively consistent.

Our methods may vary, our tool preferences may change, but how we care for our plants is based on the realities of how they grow. In this chapter you'll find basic information about the care and feeding of your potted plants.

A well-tended garden, whether planted in pots, in the ground, or a combination of the two, will reward the gardener with an ever-changing display of beautiful colors, textures, shapes, and scents.

AND CARE GUIDE

⚮ Equipment ⚮

I f you are already a gardener, chances are you will have all the tools you need to plant and maintain a potted garden. You aren't likely to have much use for your rakes, hoes, edgers, pitchfork, or wheelbarrow. But you may find it helpful to have a broader assortment of hand tools.

Essentials include:

⚮ A set of trowels for digging holes and scooping soil and mulch. You will need both a narrow, pointed style and one with a rounded end.

⚮ A small spade for filling large containers and digging holes in raised beds and permanent planters. The rounded poacher's spade is the perfect size.

⚮ A hand rake for weeding large pots and loosening soil in containers.

⚮ A dibble, to make holes for planting seeds and small-rooted plants.

⚮ All-purpose pruners. The most useful has two cutting blades and swivel handles for comfort. Always buy the highest-quality pruners you can afford and make an effort to keep them clean and sharp.

⚮ A sharp garden knife for cutting roots when potting up plants.

⚮ Loppers for branches more than half an inch (1.5cm) in diameter.

⚮ A watering can. The long-spouted, galvanized cans are especially sturdy and useful for reaching hanging baskets, wall-mounted containers, and plants at the back of a grouping. You will need a rose head for delicate seedlings and plants. If weight is a problem, use a plastic can, but don't let it freeze.

⚮ A hose and adjustable nozzle, unless your potted garden is limited to a windowsill or balcony.

⚮ A broom for sweeping up after potting and pruning.

Optional tools include:

⚮ A bulb planter. A short-handled version of this cylindrical tool is probably all you will need for container planting. Look for one with depth markings on the side.

⚮ A pair of floral snips. These are useful not only for cutting blooms but also for deadheading.

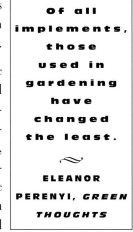

Of all implements, those used in gardening have changed the least.

⚮

ELEANOR PERENYI, *GREEN THOUGHTS*

Successful gardeners find it enormously helpful to keep their tools together in a handy container like a small paint bucket. A bowl of decorative rocks and a tin of white pebbles are useful for forcing bulbs in bowls or as decorative elements around bonsai plants. Note the bits of broken terra-cotta pot that have been saved. These remnants will be used on the bottom of a container to prevent soil from seeping out the drainage holes while still allowing water to drain well.

❧ A pair of gloves.

❧ Plant supports. Bamboo stakes in several heights, metal ring supports, linking stakes, peony rings (they work for tomatoes, too), and grid supports for floppy plants.

❧ Green twine or raffia for tying plants to stakes, trellising, or fencing.

❧ A sprayer for applying pesticides or fertilizer. Always read labels carefully, follow directions exactly, and wear protective clothing and gloves when using pesticides.

A potting bench is a wonderful luxury for any gardener, whether it's a custom-crafted teak affair with hooks and shelves for all your tools, or merely a shelf hidden away in a corner of the garden with stacks of pots and a pile of potting soil underneath.

An alternative is a small table in the garage or potting shed or on the back porch. A tiny patio or rooftop garden might have a utility area behind a screen or a group of plants where tools, extra pots, and storage bins of potting mix and fertilizer can be kept out of sight.

It's important that tools be well maintained—cleaned regularly and repaired or replaced when broken; cutting tools must be kept sharpened.

⮑ Soil ⮐

While there are limits to improving the soil in your garden beds, the soil you use for potted plants will be as good as you make it. You have complete control. Simply mix up a batch of potting soil and put it in the pots.

Keep in mind that the ideal soil for potted plants will take up nutrients and retain moisture, but will still allow oxygen to reach the plants' roots. The amount of air available to the roots is crucial to vigorous growth.

Commercial potting soil is readily available in bags from garden centers and will serve most purposes. Some potting mixes are soilless, made from decomposed compost, bark, or peat. Others use various combinations of soil, peat, vermiculite or perlite, and sand. The more peat, vermiculite, or perlite you use, the lighter the mix will be. This is especially helpful when pots must be moved around and for containers on rooftops or balconies where weight is an important consideration.

In order to supply your plants with the nutrients they need to flourish, you might add a time-release fertilizer to your potting mix. Well-aged manure in small quantities, bloodmeal, and bonemeal will supply additional nutrients.

Other good soil amendments include limestone or small amounts of wood ash for plants that prefer an alkaline soil; add coffee grounds, decomposed pine needles, leaf mold, or sulphur to increase soil acidity. By experimenting with various formulas and making adjustments, you'll find a general mix that works best for your needs.

For very dry areas, in time of drought, or for those who may not always be able to water potted plants, the addition of water-retentive materials to the potting mix may help. These gelatinous granules will help the soil retain moisture longer, but are not a substitute for regular watering.

Using soil from the garden should be avoided, especially if plants will be brought indoors at any time. Soil-dwelling insects, plant diseases, or toxins may be present. Pests and diseases might also be introduced when infected plants are added to a container. If a damaging fungus, bacteria or disease is discovered, start over after removing the infected plants, discarding the contaminated soil and disinfecting the pot with a good scrubbing using a mild solution of detergent and bleach.

This detail from a Ming Dynasty vase illustrates the ritual of watering tea plants. Today, some gardeners have substituted the wooden watering contraptions with computerized timers, underground sprinkler systems, and irrigation schemes. Old-fashioned watering cans and hand-held nozzles on the end of rubber hoses do just fine for most.

YOU CAN EASILY MAKE YOUR OWN POTTING MIX. HERE ARE A FEW FORMULAS. THE FIRST TWO RECIPES MAKE AN ESPECIALLY GOOD, WELL-DRAINED SOIL.

1 part commercial potting soil
1 part thoroughly decomposed compost
1 part coarse sand
1 part peat moss
or
2 parts peat moss
1 part vermiculite
1 part coarse sand

⮑

FOR A RICHER SOIL THAT IS STILL LIGHT AND WILL DRAIN WELL:

2 parts topsoil
1 part compost
1 part coarse sand
1 part peat moss
1 part vermiculite

⮑

THIS RECIPE IS DESIGNED FOR PLANTS THAT ARE "HEAVY FEEDERS."

1 part commercial potting soil
1 part compost
1 part vermiculite, perlite, or coarse sand

❦ Potting and Repotting ❧

One of the keys to success when potting plants is to give them a thorough watering immediately beforehand. Plunge small pots into a big tub of water, soak a flat of annuals with a fine, continuous spray, or train a slow trickle of water from the hose on a tree or shrub root-ball until it is very damp. If you plan to use terra-cotta pots, give them a good soaking too.

While the plants are soaking, prepare your pots, making sure they are scrupulously clean and that there are adequate drainage holes. Reject any pots without drainage holes, or use them as cachepots or covers for other, more suitable containers.

Add a layer of drainage material—gravel, stones, broken crockery, even Styrofoam packing peanuts (as long as they are not the biodegradable variety)—and a layer of potting mix. Water thoroughly.

Remove the plants to be potted from their containers and check the condition of the roots. If the roots are tightly packed and wrapped around themselves, loosen them by cutting down along the sides of the root mass, then gently pull the roots apart. If a plant's roots have come through the drainage holes of its original pot, cut them off before beginning the potting process.

Place the plant on top of the potting mix and cover the roots with more soil. Tap the pot on a hard surface a few times to settle the soil, adding more if needed. The top of the root mass should be about ¼ inch (6mm) below the soil. Water again until water runs from the drainage holes.

When planting a large container with a number of plants, follow the same sequence of steps as above, but add more soil so you will actually excavate some when you plant. Place the plants in their original containers in the larger pot so you can see how they will look, making design adjustments if you need to. Then remove the largest plant from its container, pruning the roots if necessary, and press the bottom of that container into the soil to make a planting hole. Place the plant in the hole, and repeat the process for each of the plants. Finally, add enough potting mix so the roots are

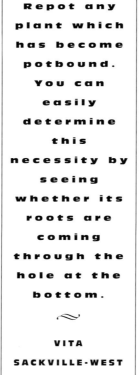

Repot any plant which has become potbound. You can easily determine this necessity by seeing whether its roots are coming through the hole at the bottom.

❦

VITA SACKVILLE-WEST

covered. Press down gently on the soil, then water thoroughly and add more soil if needed. Use the same technique to plant window boxes and wall-hanging containers.

A large permanent planter or raised bed might also be planted in this fashion, or it can be treated more like a garden bed by filling it with soil, then excavating planting holes with a small spade, trowel, or bulb planter.

When planting perennials, shrubs, or trees, providing adequate space for root growth is essential. Annuals, on the other hand, don't seem to mind living in cramped quarters.

To repot plants, follow the same steps as the original potting process. When a plant has outgrown its pot, prepare a new one, just one size larger, with drainage material and potting mix. Soak the plant in water, remove it gently from its pot and loosen the roots, removing any broken crockery or stones that have become entangled. Place the plant in the new pot and spread the roots out. Add more soil, water, tap the pot to settle the soil, and adjust the soil level to about ¼ inch (6mm) above the root mass. Water again.

Finish the potting by adding a topdressing of red gravel, white pebbles, fine bark mulch, or moss for decorative purposes and to help retain moisture.

A healthy plant is off to a good start in a ceramic pot with the addition of rich, moist potting soil. Though a satisfying chore, potting up plants can be messy. Some gardeners prefer to work on a tarp or lay down newspapers to ensure easy cleanup.

Planting a Wire Basket

A porch, terrace, balcony, pergola, or garden room seems undressed without a complement of baskets hanging from the ceilings and walls. Some gardeners purchase ready-made hanging gardens from plant centers and nurseries. Others prefer to create their own, using little more than wire baskets, moss, and creativity.

Wire baskets come in a wide variety of shapes and sizes ranging from deep and rounded to small and conical to half-round ones (for walls). Most are designed to be seen from below or head-on, an important consideration from a design aspect.

Select plants that are compatible in their soil, light, and watering needs. You'll also want to use plants that cascade nicely, especially for the sides and bottom of the basket. Impatiens, lobelia, alyssum, petunias, vinca, and ivy work well. Look for lively contrasts in textures, colors, and shapes from begonias, variegated ivy, scented geraniums, portulaca, Swan River daisies, and pansies, among many others.

While a wire basket of plants is relatively easy to assemble, it does require some time and the work should be done all at once to avoid dried-out plants.

Prepare the plants by soaking them. In the meantime, soak sheets of moss which will be used to line the exterior of the basket. When the moss is saturated, take a handful and squeeze it until it no longer drips. Turn the basket upside down and fit the moss between two wires, wrapping a bit around the wires. It will stay in place on its own. Continue to wrap the basket evenly in the moss until it is covered. Invert the basket and rest it on a large-mouthed flowerpot or bowl.

You may want to line a moss-covered basket with an interior liner which allows water to pass through, but retains soil. Commercial liners available at garden centers or a piece of mulch cloth cut to size will serve this purpose.

Fill the basket with potting mix. Then carefully poke holes through the moss and liner material. You may need a small tool—a knitting needle, knife, or stick—to cut through the liner. Insert a plant in the hole and allow the soil to close around it. Plant all the way around the basket, including the bottom. Fill the top of the basket, too. Add chains or rope for hanging, hang the basket on its hook or support, and water it thoroughly.

∽ Water ∽

It almost goes without saying: plants need water to survive. Some plants, like succulents and cacti, will survive with minimal water. Others, particularly annuals and vegetables, must be watered daily, or more often in extremely hot, windy, and dry conditions.

You will know that your pots need watering if, when you put your finger about an inch or two (2.5 to 5cm) into the soil, you find it dry. Test the soil in larger, deep containers by excavating a small hole about 6 inches (15cm) down.

In hot summer weather, you will probably have to water outdoor plants every day unless it has rained. Watering in the morning allows plants to make use of the moisture during the day. The danger of watering at night is that the moisture may attract slugs and other pests, and the roots might also sit too long in the water, promoting disease.

Several trips with a watering can will fill the requirements of a small balcony or patio garden. A more substantial potted garden is better served by a hose with a multifunction nozzle. Owners of large permanent planters and raised beds might consider installing an irrigation system that can be very sophisticated, with timed devices, or as simple as soaker hoses buried in the beds. These are easiest to install when the beds are first made.

Watering hanging baskets and window boxes can sometimes pose logistical problems, so it is well to take that into consideration when positioning them.

If you plan to be away during the growing season, be sure to make plant-sitting arrangements. For a short-term reprieve, move particularly vulnerable plants to a sheltered shady spot to reduce watering needs. Small terra-cotta pots can be placed on a tray of gravel and water to provide additional moisture. And you can add moisture-retentive granules to the soil.

A word on houseplants: take care not to overwater. Although heated interiors can have a drying effect on foliage, an indoor plant's roots will quickly rot if it is watered too frequently. Use the finger-in-the-soil test rather than a schedule to determine when you water. Water houseplants until the water begins to drain out from the drainage holes.

❧ Fertilizer ❧

Vita Sackville-West was fond of gardening in pots and enjoyed great success. Perhaps one of the reasons for her mastery was the attention she paid to feeding her potted plants.

She wrote in one of her *Observer* columns, "Plants in pots naturally exhaust the soil they are planted in, and need replenishment. They have nothing else to draw on, and must depend on us, their owners, for the nourishment they cannot obtain for themselves. Our responsibility is great towards these beautiful imaginations of nature, so pathetically and helplessly at our command."

While we might not all see our potted plants as pathetic and helpless, Vita was correct when she pointed out that sufficient plant nutrition is an essential step to successful container gardening. Even if you've started out with the best-quality potting mix, your plants will soon use up the nutrients and will be hungry for more. Pots which require frequent watering, whether due to the type of plants, the small size of the pot, or the weather, will be depleted of nutrients at a faster rate than those which are watered less frequently.

Applications of commercial fertilizers will likely meet the nutritional needs of nearly all of your potted plants.

Fertilizers are readily available at garden and agricultural centers, hardware stores, and some general purpose stores. You'll find fish emulsions, manure- or seaweed-based mixtures, and any number of combinations of nitrogen, phosphate, and potassium that make up most commercially sold fertilizers.

The numbers on the bag refer to the percentages, by weight, of each of the three elements. So a 5-10-10 fertilizer will have 5 percent nitrogen, and 10 percent each phosphate and potassium (sometimes called potash). There are also time-release fertilizers which slowly release nutrients over the course of several months. These are most often added to the soil at potting time.

While every plant has different needs, there are a few general rules of thumb to follow. For example, foliage plants will need a fertilizer with a high nitrogen level. Flowering annuals, perennials, and strawberries do better when the ratios of nitrogen to potassium are about the same. Citrus trees will need more iron than other plants. Succulents do best with low levels of nutrients. Orchids, roses,

rhododendrons, azaleas, and many evergreens, because of their appetite for iron, are acid-loving plants while iris, clematis, tomatoes, and melons prefer "sweet," or alkaline, soil.

Burdening plants with excess nitrogen is one of the most common gardening mistakes. It will cause weak, spindly growth, "burning," and even death. A slow-release feeding of nitrogen will minimize the danger. If your plants are deficient in nitrogen, they will appear yellowed.

Insufficient phosphorus in the soil in your pots will reduce growth, cause thin stems, reduced flowering, and loss of lower leaves. Potassium-deficient soil will also reduce growth, diminish root systems, and produce burned-looking leaf edges and a wilted appearance.

In addition to standard fertilizers, there are many specialty fertilizers on the market, designed to meet the needs of rhododendrons, azaleas, roses, or vegetables. While these can be helpful, especially to the novice gardener, they are generally very expensive. You may find that once you get to know your plants' requirements, you will be able to use standard fertilizers in the formula that works best.

Organic fertilizers like manure, compost, or bloodmeal are excellent sources of nutrients, but take a fairly long time to break down and release their nutrients. They may be best used in the original potting mix.

Potted plants often need a "quick fix." Water-soluble fertilizers, some already in liquid form, others that come ready-to-mix, are efficient for delivering the frequent "meals" potted plants

When selecting a fertilizer for the potted garden, it's important to read the label carefully in order to determine the percentages of nitrogen, phosphorous, and potassium it contains. The organic fertilizer pictured below has 5 percent nitrogen, 3 percent phosphorous, and 5 percent potassium. A higher phosphorous level, perhaps 10 percent, would be best for new plantings that need a boost for their root development.

Regular watering with a small dose of fertilizer will keep these Marguerite chrysanthemums, ivy-leaf geraniums, and cyclamen blooming prolifically all summer.

crave. You may want to feed your plants, especially heavy-flowering annuals and vegetables, every week. Herbaceous plants in large containers might be fertilized every other or every third week.

Rosemarie Vassalluzzo, the Grand Sweepstakes Winner at the famous Philadelphia Flower Show for twelve consecutive years, and whose success with potted plants is legendary, always keeps "a drop" of standard, commercial, water-soluble fertilizer in her watering cans, giving her plants a small dose of nutrients with each watering. A quarter teaspoon (5ml) of fertilizer to one gallon (3.8L) of water is a good formula to follow for creating a mixture that helps plants thrive.

Trees and shrubs, as long as they are in sufficiently large containers, should be fed on a regular schedule, but not until the soil has been tested for pH and nutrient levels. Once the condition of the soil is pinpointed, you'll know more precisely what fertilizer ratio to use.

Potted plants will also benefit from applications of foliar fertilizer. This form of liquid fertilizer is sprayed directly onto the plant's leaves, which absorb the nutrients directly. Avoid foliar feeding on sunny days because it may burn the leaves.

❧ Pruning ❧

Although the thought of it terrifies even some of the most experienced gardeners, pruning is relatively simple. Gardeners prune trees, shrubs, roses, and sometimes perennials to remove dead or damaged plant parts, restrict growth, improve the plant's shape, encourage new growth and flowering, and increase fruiting.

Entire books have been written about pruning, and there are specific techniques for various types of plants. There are, however, a few basics.

❧ Always use very sharp, clean pruners, loppers, or shears for pruning your plants. A dull blade will damage the plant, and a dirty one might introduce disease.

❧ Use alcohol to clean pruners after each pruning cut from a diseased tree or shrub.

❧ Remove a dead, dying, damaged, crossed, or weak branch with a clean, angled cut at the point where it is attached to the parent stem or to a lateral side branch.

> Let the light in, and the air.... Terrified though we may be of cutting inexpertly into living wood, or of cutting at the wrong time, the most inexperienced amongst us need have no fear in chopping away dead rubbish which Nature herself has discarded.
>
> ❧
>
> **VITA SACKVILLE-WEST ON PRUNING**

❧ Prune the roots of potbound plants when transplanting to encourage new growth.

❧ Always prune back to a bud or an intersecting branch because new growth is most likely to take place from a bud.

❧ Avoid leaving stumps, which can rot and invite infection.

❧ Prune to thin out foliage and allow more sun and air to reach interior branches. Thinning cuts are often made just above ground level on shrubs.

❧ Most shrubs that bloom in the spring can be pruned after they have flowered.

❧ Prune evergreens, except conifers, in winter or very early spring to reduce the size, to shape, or to remove dead, diseased, or damaged wood.

❧ Most broad-leafed evergreens, such as rhododendrons and azaleas, rarely need pruning except to remove dead flowers, damaged branches, or, in the case of hollies, to shape.

Pruning to remove dead or damaged growth keeps plants such as this dwarf evergreen healthy. If trees and shrubs that have been genetically bred or grafted to be dwarfed are selected for container gardening, little pruning, other than that needed to keep the plant thriving, will be necessary.

Pruning Roses

All roses need pruning to ensure proper growth, and to encourage large blooms. Hybrid tea, grandiflora, and floribunda types should be pruned every spring after danger of frost. Cut out all dead, diseased, or damaged wood; remove canes that rub against other canes; and prune out the oldest cane each year. You will also want to cut back the remaining canes, based on the type of rose. Refer to one of the specialty books listed in the suggested reading (page 118) for specifics.

Rose standards should be cut back in the spring to a rounded shape about 8 to 10 inches (20 to 25cm) from the base of the crown. Prune climbing roses in the fall just before the weather turns cold by cutting out dead or diseased wood and removing the two oldest canes. Shorten the side branches by about 6 inches (15cm) after they flower.

Miniature or patio roses don't need much in the way of pruning, but will do best when dead blooms are removed after flowering and hips are removed in the spring.

Planting a Strawberry Jar

A strawberry jar, usually made of unadorned terra-cotta, but sometimes glazed, is an urn-shaped container with pocket-shaped openings scattered over its surface. These pockets have traditionally been planted with strawberries, which grow happily in the jars, producing fruit that dangles down the sides.

Creative gardeners also pack their strawberry jars with dense cascading herbs like thyme, oregano, and caraway. Nasturtiums, with their rich, hot colors, look especially lovely draped around a strawberry jar. Impatiens, portulaca, sedums, lobelia, alyssum, wax or tuberous begonias, and petunias are also suitable candidates to complement strawberry jars.

Planting a strawberry jar involves the same steps as planting any other container, except that the openings on the sides must be dealt with. An easy method is to work a level at a time, placing a piece of burlap or other loosely woven fabric over each hole before adding the soil, so that each section is filled like an individual pot.

Once the jar is filled with soil, remove the fabric from a hole (you may need to pull it with a crochet hook or pin), scoop out a little soil using your other hand to retain the space, and plant your seedling. Repeat the process until you have filled each pocket, then plant the top. Water thoroughly and be prepared for some soil to escape until the roots grow.

OPPOSITE: *Some broadleaf evergreens, especially boxwood, and many roses benefit from an overcoat of burlap in preparation for frigid winter weather. Potted plants may be wrapped, container and all, with an inner layer of dry leaves for insulation. Anti-desiccant sprays applied to magnolia, mahonia, holly and other broadleaf evergreens will protect the plants from moisture-robbing winter winds.*

Winter Protection for Potted Trees and Shrubs

Trees and shrubs in containers are indeed particularly vulnerable to damage from the cold. While their cousins in the garden enjoy the protection of the even temperature of below-ground soil, cold winds and freezing weather can kill potted roots in a short time.

> Of course you realize that a plant in a pot is far more vulnerable to frost than a plant in the ground.
>
> ~
>
> VITA SACKVILLE-WEST

Vita Sackville-West, although she lived in Kent where the winters are mild, worried about potted plants. "Many people grow hydrangeas or fuchsias in tubs, and are puzzled to know what to do about them through the horrible months we have ahead of us," she wrote in a December column. She suggested that her readers "wrap the pots round with any warm covering you can get, straw or bracken; of if your pots are not too large, sink them into a bed of ashes up to the rim. That will prevent the frost from getting at them."

There are other methods for protecting potted plants that don't involve large amounts of ashes. Plants in raised beds and permanent planters will benefit from a thick layer of mulch and a blanket of evergreen branches once the weather has turned very cold. This will prevent the freeze-thaw-freeze cycle from damaging the plants.

Move tender deciduous trees and shrubs into a garage, shed, or unheated porch. You may need to water occasionally. Potted plants on a terrace, patio, or rooftop have a better chance at survival if you huddle them close together in a corner and up against a sheltering wall. Bales of hay or plastic bags filled with dry leaves or Styrofoam nestled around the pots will help, as will wrapping the pots in "bubble-wrap" sheeting or burlap.

PLANTS

With the thousands of cultivated plants
available to gardeners, how does one narrow the
selection to just a few for pots on the terrace or
balcony? Poring over catalogs, design books, horticultural references, and gardening
magazines is a start. Visiting open gardens,
arboretums, garden centers, and garden shows
helps build a body of knowledge. And sharing
information with gardening friends gives
it all a personal touch. But knowing the right
plant for the right place frequently results as
much from lucky chance as from expertise.
In this section, you'll find suggestions for plant
choices that have worked well for others. Some
will work for you. Others won't at all, but
might further your search for a variety or cultivar
that is just what you are looking for.
In the Sources section, you will find
a listing of nurseries and mail-order companies
for many of the plants listed here.

Full-blown heads of pink hydrangea are contained
in a highly decorative raised container. The pink of
the blooms is in startling contrast with the grays and
greens of the tropical setting behind them.

FOR POTS

ᐱ Trees and Shrubs ᐱ

Trees and shrubs are the backbone of the garden. Their strong lines and sturdy limbs become the "bones" of the garden, while all the other plants add muscle and flesh.

Evergreen trees and shrubs provide a backdrop for a three-season parade of foliage and flowers, then, when other plants have retired, these stalwarts supply the winter garden with green "architecture." Deciduous trees and shrubs, those which lose their leaves each fall, add shape, color, and texture, often with spectacular shows of changing flowers and foliage, and occasionally striking exfoliating bark or pigmented twigs.

When buying trees and shrubs, look for a container-grown plant rather than one that has been field-grown; it won't have had its root system disturbed and will not need drastic pruning to accommodate a reduced root-to-top ratio. Also look for trees that have not been staked—if a tree is staked, it won't be able stand up on its own. (Dwarf fruit trees are an exception to this rule.)

The key to success in planting trees and shrubs in pots is selecting species and varieties that are suited for life in a container. The few listed here have proved their value in the potted garden time after time. For other species, visit nurseries and garden centers, or consult some of the books in the suggested reading.

RIGHT: *Gardeners should not be intimidated by the prospect of growing trees in containers, but they should keep in mind that many trees will grow to towering heights. The birch pictured here, for example, could reach 100 feet (30m) at maturity. The handsome river birch (*Betula nigra *'Heritage'), however, will grow to only about 30 feet (9m).*

OPPOSITE, TOP: *Many of the spruce varieties are good prospects for containers, particularly low-growing cultivars. The 'Fat Albert' variety of the Colorado blue spruce reaches 10 feet (3m) in as many years.*

OPPOSITE, BOTTOM: Berberis thunbergii, *or Japanese barberry, provides rich red foliage in the garden and will grow happily in containers. Dwarf varieties like 'Crimson Pygmy' grow to about three feet (90cm).*

Deciduous Trees

❧ Japanese maple (*Acer palmatum*)—One of the most beautiful trees for containers, its leaves are red, green, yellow-green, or variegated white with pink. A slow grower with ultimate height of 20 feet (6m). Will grow in light shade, but colors are richest in full sun. Avoid hot, dry winds.

❧ Birch (*Betula*)—Because of a variety of pests and diseases, birch does best in areas with cold winters. Often clump-growing, sometimes weeping, they will adapt to life in large containers on terraces or rooftops.

❧ Crape myrtle (*Lagerstroemia*)—Not hardy in very cold areas, and sometimes evergreen. A small tree, often clump-growing, it produces a profusion of pink, mauve, purple, red, or white flowers all summer.

❧ Crab apple (*Malus* hybrids)—Grown as both weeping and upright specimens, the ornamental crab apple has pretty pink or white flowers in early spring and showy yellow or red fruits in fall.

❧ Cherry (*Prunus*)—Also grown as weeping or upright trees, ornamental cherries are spectacular in spring, when they are covered in lovely pink blooms.

Evergreen Trees

❧ Juniper (*Juniperus*)—Junipers are extraordinarily versatile in the potted garden. Look for juniper varieties, including blue-green, 12-foot (3.7m) 'Columnar', and 'Pfitzerana', which reaches 5 feet (1.5m) and has green leaves with yellow tips.

❧ Pine (*Pinus*)—There are many varieties suitable for the potted garden. Some special performers include black pine (*P. thunbergii*), which grows up to 10 feet (3m) and will tolerate windy conditions; Scotch pine (*P. sylvestris*); and Japanese white pine (*P. parviflora*), a slow-growing type which will eventually reach 10 feet (3m).

❧ Yew (*Taxus*)—A useful evergreen that will grow in shade, *Taxus baccata* will reach about 10 feet (3m). Some well-known cultivars include *T. b.* 'Fastigiata', or Irish yew, and *T. b.* 'Fastigiata Aurea,' which features striking yellow-margined leaves.

❧ False cypress (*Chamaecyparis*)—A range of attractive evergreen trees (and shrubs) with beautiful, feathery foliage in varying shades of greens, including pale chartreuse.

🌿 Arborvitae (*Thuja*)—Several varieties can be grown in pots and are often used as windbreaks and screens.

🌿 Spruce (*Picea*)—The dwarf Alberta spruce (*P. glauca* 'Conica')is one of the most commonly used potted evergreens.

Deciduous Shrubs

🌿 Angel's trumpet (*Brugmansia*)—A small, showy tender tree with spectacular trumpet-shaped white, yellow, pink, or red flowers which dangle from its branches.

🌿 Barberry (*Berberis*)—Small red leaves, grows up to 6 feet (1.8m) but can be kept smaller with pruning. Prefers sun.

🌿 Blue spirea (*Caryopteris*)—Beautiful blue flowers in August or September on a small 2- to 3-foot (60 to 90cm) shrub.

🌿 Hydrangea (*Hydrangea*)—Many varieties, including lace-cap, oak-leafed, and hortensia types. Flowers are white, shades of blue, pink, or red. Soils high in acid will produce intense blue flowers.

🌿 Hypericum (*Hypericum*)—Useful small, rounded shrub growing up to about 3 feet (90cm) with attractive yellow flowers.

🌿 Butterfly bush (*Buddleia*)—A vigorous sub shrub with huge white, dark to light purple, or pink flower heads. Should be cut back in the fall. Look for dwarf varieties.

Evergreen Shrubs

🌿 Rhododendron (*Rhododendron*)—Hundreds of varieties. Choose one of the dwarf or compact types. Showy flowers come in shades of red, pink, white, lavender, and yellow. Prefer an acid soil and moist conditions.

🌿 Azalea (*Azalea*)—Hundreds of varieties, including many small, compact, and dwarf ones. Some are deciduous. Likes an acid soil.

🌿 Daphne (*Daphne*)—Several varieties, some quite dwarf, known for small, attractive variegated leaves and highly scented blooms.

🌿 Boxwood (*Buxus sempervirens*)—Slow-growing, bushy shrubs with small, shiny oval leaves. Excellent for shaping.

🌿 Viburnum (*Viburnum*)—Some evergreen varieties, others are deciduous. Select dwarf or compact varieties. Bushy, strong growers, intensely scented flowers, fall fruits.

🌿 Juniper, pine, yew, arborvitae, and spruce varieties.

❧ Perennials ❧

Gardeners who grow perennials know the joy of greeting their emerging plants each spring after the plants' essential winter rest. Year after year the perennials reward us with their flowers, often for an all-too-brief, but breathtakingly beautiful, time.

Most perennials will grow well in containers. They may make a few more demands, perhaps be a tiny bit more difficult. But their splendor makes every extra effort worthwhile.

If you have favorite perennials in your borders, by all means try them in pots. If roses are your passion, add a few in containers to your terrace. If lilies are your first choice, plant as many as you can in elegant ornamental pots.

Grow astilbes, *Brunnera macrophylla*, pulmonaria, bergenia, lady's mantle, and violas in a corner of the patio where the sun is filtered through a canopy of trees. In a bright, sunny spot on a deck or patio, plant big tubs of lilies, euphorbias, sedums, violas, hardy geraniums, iris, daylilies, or peonies.

Aim for a succession of blooms. The garden's show might open with some bulbs, Jacob's ladder, violas, and forget-me-nots followed closely by bleeding hearts, primulas, and gentians. Poppies, iris, and some of the daisies might be the next performers with foxglove and sweet William waiting in the wings. A long-running show will proceed with peonies, roses, perennial geraniums, lilies, daylilies, veronicas, phlox, and asters.

Salvias, which are in the sage family, are enormously useful in the potted garden. Especially showy, with some growing to the size of a large shrub in one season, are the Mexican and South American varieties, including *Salvia uliginosa*, *S. cacaliifolia*, and *S. patens*. They are tender, so you'll need to cut them back and bring them in for the winter.

Plant a stone trough with tiny, mound-forming or creeping plants like dianthus varieties, thrift (*Armeria*), *Campanula carpatica*, gentian, miniature hosta, lamium, potentilla, or some of the smaller sedums.

Build a collection of species chrysthanthemums, veronicas, or daylilies. Try Japanese iris for the first time or see if lupines will grow for you.

Look for new colors or forms. Don't limit yourself to the tried and true. Experiment!

❧ Annuals ❧

Annuals and bedding plants are the workhorses of the potted garden—uncomplicated, needing little attention, present for strong color and full foliage. They give their all during their brief lives, then with the first frost, they're gone, only to be replaced by the next generation come spring.

The choice of annuals is staggering. Every shade of every color. Compact to climbing. Showy or discreet. There are the old reliables—wax begonias, impatiens, geraniums,, ageratum, petunias, and marigolds—so common as to be ubiquitious, yet lovely, despite their plebian nature. With minimal effort, success is nearly guaranteed.

The challenge to the container gardener is to experiment with new varieties, untried combinations, and unfamilar plants.

FAR RIGHT: A relatively easy vine to grow in pots, Akebia quinata is a woody-stemmed twining vine with unusual purple to pink flowers appearing in late spring. Given a trellis, wires, or posts to climb, it will reach up to 30 feet (9m) tall.

RIGHT: Nearly every gardener has had some experience with annuals in pots. While the old reliables may be the first that come to mind, there are dozens of species, like the lovely gazania, that deserve more notice.

Keeping a watchful eye on horticultural developments and an open mind about annuals will ensure that your potted garden is never a dull place.

Half-hardy plants, tender perennials, and some bulbs are often treated as annuals in colder climates where the plants won't survive a winter outdoors but are easily replaced the following year. Gardeners who long for the dramatic beauty of delphiniums, but are regularly disappointed by their failure to survive, might consider growing them as annuals, replanting with strong seedlings each spring. Lavatara, or tree mallow, a gorgeous, bushy, tender perennial with very large white or rose-colored hibiscuslike blooms, makes a great show as an annual grown from seed or seedlings in northern gardens. Though they will become small trees in mild climates, fuchsias are often grown as annuals where winters are cold.

Heliotrope, *Felicia* (blue marguerite), *Gomphrena* (globe amaranth), gazania, lantana, *Osteospermum*, verbena, nicotiana, various daisies (including *Argyranthemum frutescens*), and African daisy are all worthy of consideration in pots, whether alone as showy statements or mixed with compatible cousins.

Annuals and bedding plants can be grown with little effort. Regular deadheading is a must with these plants. By removing spent blossoms you will prevent the production of seed, thus allowing the plant to put all its energies into producing more flowers for you to enjoy. A healthy dose of fertilizer every week or so will give the plants the food they need to flower till frost.

⤳ Vines ⤳

Overlooked far too often in garden schemes, vines can perform several functions and are especially useful in potted gardens because of their vertical inclinations. Vines are often decorative, adding color, shape, and texture to walls, fences, railings, lampposts, and other structures. They are also valuable as background plantings, setting a rich, green stage for shrubs, perennials, or annuals. Thick climbers like grape, Persian ivy, silver lace vine, Virginia creeper, and hops will shade a wall or terrace and are useful as screens, disguising unsightly views or architectural flaws.

Smaller vines—morning glory, porcelain berry, sweet peas, or the exotic mandevilla—add height and architectural interest, along with lovely color, to a deck, patio, or paved area when planted in a pot with a good sturdy trellis or a tripod of bamboo poles.

Most vines will grow happily in containers. Large perennial woody species, like wisteria, trumpet vine, bouganvillea, Carolina jasmine, climbing fig or hydrangea, honeysuckle, and silver lace vine, will require large quarters—an oversize tub, barrel, or permanent planter—in order to survive. Annual vines, including morning glory, hyacinth bean, Japanese hops, scarlet runner bean, and cathedral bells, will not need as much space.

Clematis, among the most beautiful of vines, is not the most enthusiastic pot dweller, although gardeners who provide an alkaline soil, plenty of mulch or lush underplantings to keep the roots cool, and enough sun to encourage foliage and flower growth, will be rewarded with incomparable beauty. The autumn-blooming variety (*Clematis paniculata*) is one of the easiest clematis to grow and is also blessed with an exquisite honey scent.

In order to provide the right kind of support for vines in your potted garden, you must first determine how they climb. Passionflower, clematis, grape, and sweet pea, for example, send out clinging tendrils from their stems. The tendrils will wrap around mesh netting or a grid of wires attached to a wall or fence, standard, or custom-designed trellising or stakes.

Twining vines wrap themselves around their support. Examples include wisteria, honeysuckle, and akebia. These plants will twine right up a stake, wire, pole, trellising, arbor, open-structured fencing, or column.

LEFT: *Though sometimes difficult to get started, clematis vines will grow well in pots when their needs are met. These regal vines have been bred for nearly infinite variety, including the lavender 'P.T. James' (shown here), pink and white 'Nelly Moser', 'Henryi' (a pure white), 'Jackmanii' (deepest purple), and C. florida 'Sieboldii', an exotic white with purple centers that resembles the passionflower.*

A third type of climber are those which grow little suction cup–like devices from their stems. These adhesive disks attach themselves to the support, most often a wall or fence. Boston ivy, Virginia creeper, and cross vine climb this way.

Another way vines grow is with rootlike holdfasts, which are actually aerial roots that cling to walls and can put deteriorating mortar at risk for further damage. However, if a brick or stone wall is solid and repointed when needed, climbing vines pose no danger. Ivy, trumpet vine, and climbing hydrangea climb with these aerial roots.

Be sure the support you provide is sturdy enough for the vines you grow. Wisteria, honeysuckle, trumpet vine, akebia, Boston ivy, Virginia creeper, and climbing hydrangea will need strong supports because of their vigor.

BELOW: *A lush garden is studded with wooden supports for climbing plants. Annual vines are useful for filling in a spot in the garden while a young tree or other tall element becomes established.*

RIGHT: *Morning glories are among the easiest vines to grow. Before sowing the seeds indoors in late spring, nick them with sandpaper or a nail file and fold them in damp toweling overnight. This increases the rate of germination.*

⌘ Herbs ⌘

An essential for the gourmet chef, herbs in pots are also beloved by gardeners who yearn for interesting textures, shapes, scents, and colors. Nearly any herb cultivated in the vegetable garden or the herbacious border can be grown in a container.

Herb plants are as diverse as any other group, with annual, perennial, biennial, and bulbous species, each with its own cultural requirements. In general, herbs are not fussy about soil, although most do not tolerate wet conditions. Nearly all require full sun to thrive.

Uses of herbs in the potted garden abound. Plant a big tub, strawberry jar, or hanging wire basket with culinary herbs like parsley, thyme, sage, oregano, chives, and basil and put it within easy reach of the kitchen.

Lavender in its many varieties is a magnificent addition to the potted garden. A stately row of it soaking up the summer sun in massive terra-cotta pots will make you feel as if you were in Provence. Pinch off a few leaves to add to a summer bath or save the clippings, after you've given them a post-bloom shearing, to toss on the fire in winter—the smoke will perfume the entire house.

A broad cement or terra-cotta bowl packed with brilliant orange calendula is a cheerful summer sight, with the added benefit of petals which can be used like saffron to flavor foods or to add a spicy lift to salads.

Parsley, especially the dense, curly type, is a delightful foliage foil for intensely colored, tall or spiky flowers. Use it as an underplanting for daffodils, lilies, veronicas, salvia, foxglove, or standards of fuchsia, heliotrope, lantana, or rose.

Fennel, with its feathery wands of green or bronzed purple, is useful as a background foliage plant, as is dill, with its finely cut bright green leaves. Dill will also produce huge, round chartreuse flower heads on tall stalks. The finely lobed blue-green leaves of meadow rue, which grow in rounded clumps, are effective as foliage partners with a morning glory vine and pots of chives, sage, golden oregano, parsley, or purple salvia.

Basils, of which there are dozens of cultivars, and sage, which ranges from silver to purple to a rich cream and green variegation, grow well in pots and are good for cooking or just to admire. Creeping thyme varieties supply culinary delight

and make an attractive, aromatic, low-growing underplanting.

Some herbs are most noticeable for their flowers. Think of chives for their round, pink flowers, or borage, which produces bright blue pendant flowers and will grow to about 3 feet (90cm) from seeds sown in the spring. Nasturtiums, often grown as an herb, have brilliant orange, cream, scarlet, yellow, and red cuplike flowers which stand out from the lily-pad-shaped leaves. Both the flowers, and the leaves have a peppery taste similar to watercress. Grow nasturtiums in a window box on a deck or windowsill and let them trail downward. You'll feel like you are at Giverny.

Mint, which makes such a refreshing garnish for iced tea, sorbet, or lamb, should always be grown in pots because of its invasive nature. You can raise a lush stand of spearmint, peppermint, variegated, or apple mint in a simple pot sunk into the garden or standing on the patio. Keep it cut back for a pleasing round shape and to prevent it from flowering.

The list of other herbs to grow in pots is a long one and includes Italian parsley, arugula, cilantro, rosemary, marjoram, tarragon, sorrel, chamomile, comfrey, and lemon verbena.

ABOVE: *Windowsill herb gardening is within the capabilities of nearly anyone, as herbs are relatively undemanding, requiring little more than plenty of sun and regular watering.*

LEFT, TOP: *Sage is a useful herb, both in the kitchen and in the potted garden. The purple sage pictured here has enough character to stand alone in a container.*

LEFT, BOTTOM: *Basil is a staple of the herb garden, and gardeners may choose from over a dozen varieties. The one here is a miniature purple cultivar.*

In the garden outside a Cheshire cottage, herbs predominate. Perched on a twig bench is a pot of various thymes, grown for their delightful scent, their culinary usefulness, and their range of color.

✆ Bulbs ✆

The most difficult aspect of growing daffodils is selecting which ones to grow. Most bulbs look best when planted in all-of-a-kind groups, though some gardeners have created successful compositions of mixed bulbs. While not essential, adding a small handful of bonemeal to the soil before planting a pot of bulbs can give them an extra boost for their spring performance.

Few plant families lend themselves as well to pot culture as do bulbs. Some species will have but one or two dazzling performances, while others will happily bloom for a few years, especially when planted in a loose, loamy soil and if they are dug up and divided every other year or so. The term "bulb" also loosely refers to plants which grow from corms, tubers, and rhizomes.

A rule of thumb for successful bulb growing is to always select the largest bulbs available. Bulbs in containers should be planted at least 4 or 5 inches (10 or 13cm) deep, but can be placed as close as 1 or 2 inches (2.5 or 5cm) apart, as long as they do not touch the sides of the container.

To achieve a longer bloom time, plant several layers. The first group should be planted about 7 inches (18cm) deep and covered with soil; then plant another layer at 4 or 5 inches (10 or 13cm).

Water well and protect from frost during cold winter months by covering the containers or by storing in a cool, dry place. To assure adequate drainage in the container, add a layer of gravel or broken crockery to the bottom of the pot.

Bulb experts recommend a layer of decayed leaves over the broken crockery to retain moisture and to prevent the soil from clogging the drainage after watering.

Bright, bold daffodils are the harbinger of spring, whether forced indoors in colorful glazed bowls or grown outdoors in pots on a terrace or balcony. Among the easiest bulbs to grow, daffodils are actually the large trumpet-shaped members of a large family known as narcissi, which originated in Europe. Narcissi growers have twelve official classifications including large or small-cupped, double, *Jonquilla, Tazetta, Cyclamineus,* and *Tiandrus.* Some of the more frequently grown varieties include:

- King Alfred. These are the classic big yellow trumpets in six-petal faces. Up to 18 inches (45cm) tall, they bloom in early spring.

- Mount Hood. Another trumpet type, they open as a creamy yellow and turn a soft white. Early spring bloomers on 16- to 18-inch (40 to 45cm) stems.

- Salome. A large-cupped variety, Salome starts out yellow and apricot and slowly changes to a soft pink bloom on 14- to 16-inch (35 to 40cm) stems in midspring. Grow in shade for the pink tint.

- Ice Follies. Another large-cupped narcissus, this early-bloomer has a yellow cup in a white face.

- Barrett Browning. The red-orange center of this white-faced large-cupped variety blooms in early spring.

- Tête-à-Tête. A miniature *Cyclamineus* narcissus, it grows just 6 to 8 inches (15 to 20cm) tall, with bold yellow trumpets set in swept-back petals. Very early blooming. 'Jack Snipe', a yellow trumpet with white petals, and 'Jetfire', orange-red cup with bright yellow petals, are similar cultivars.

- Petit Four. A beautiful, delicate narcissus with double apricot center in a white face, flowering in midspring.

Tulips, which originated in what is now Turkey, have been cultivated for about four hundred years. Today, most start out life in Holland and are readily available by mail order or through garden centers.

Nearly all tulips do well growing in pots, so the varieties you select are simply a matter of taste. They look best when massed in single-color groups. Some of the most sought-after types include:

❧ Darwin Hybrids. Huge, brightly colored flowers in the classic tulip shape on 20- to 24-inch (51 to 60cm) stems. Colors include pure white ('Maureen'), deep red ('Appledoorn'), golden yellow ('Golden Appledoorn'), and deep pink ('Pink Impression'). There are also striped and flame-patterned cultivars. Darwins bloom in mid- to late spring, depending on the cultivar.

❧ Lily-flowered. Tall (22 to 24 inches [56 to 60cm]) pointed petals in broad array of hues with many multicolored and candy-striped cultivars. They bloom in late spring.

❧ Peony. Also called double-late tulips, they are 18 to 20 inches (45 to 51cm) tall and bloom in late spring. Attractive cultivars include 'Angelique' (palest pink), 'Lilac Perfection' (deep lilac), and 'Mount Tacoma' (white).

Many other bulbs adapt well to pot culture. Agapanthus, or lily-of-the-Nile, is one of the most

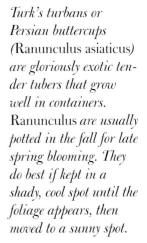

Turk's turbans or Persian buttercups (Ranunculus asiaticus) are gloriously exotic tender tubers that grow well in containers. Ranunculus are usually potted in the fall for late spring blooming. They do best if kept in a shady, cool spot until the foliage appears, then moved to a sunny spot.

❧ Triumph. Shorter (12 to 20 inches [30 to 51cm]) midspring bloomers, Triumphs are good for indoor forcing or for growing in containers outside. Colors include apricot ('Apricot Beauty'), purple ('Blue Ribbon'), deep pink ('Don Quixote'), pure white ('White Dream'), as well as striped and bicolors.

❧ Greigii. Pointed flowers on 6- to 8-inch (15 to 20cm) stems sit close to their red-striped leaves. 'Red Riding Hood', 'Golden Tango', and red and-white 'Pinocchio' are popular cultivars. These very early bloomers look elegant massed in a big, shallow bowl or stone trough.

❧ Parrot. Ruffled petals give a feathery look to these 18- to 20-inch (45 to 51cm) late spring bloomers. Parrots come in a full range of colors from white to deep maroon to multicolored.

extravagant. Reaching heights up to 5 feet (1.5m), with bright blue or white long-lasting flowers above attenuated, narrow, fleshy green leaves, it will grow in part or full sun, but its tender rhizomes must be brought indoors where temperatures drop below 26°F (-3°C).

Showy, dramatic canna lilies are rhizomatous plants which can be easily grown in containers. Growing up to 6 feet (1.8m) tall, these sun-lovers produce several flower stalks with multiple red, orange, yellow, pink, or apricot blooms in midsummer. Dwarf varieties grow 2 to 4 feet (60 to 120cm). In colder climates, store the rhizomes in a cool, dry place.

Crocus, grape hyacinth, anemone, ranunculus, tuberous begonias, clivia, crocosmia, cyclamen, lilies, tuberoses, dahlias, and oxalis are all excellent candidates for growing in pots, indoors or out.

⮷ Fruits ⮶

Lemon and lime trees, figs, and pomegranates have been grown in pots for centuries. Today, nearly any fruit grown in an orchard is a candidate for the potted garden, thanks to the development of new dwarf varieties and the miracle of grafting. Citrus trees, apples, peaches, nectarines, apricots, plums, cherries, and figs will live comfortably for years in containers. You'll want to educate yourself well on the care of dwarf, potted fruit trees because they require much more attention than other trees and shrubs.

Rhubarb and melons will do well in pots, too, given enough sun, water, and nutrients. And grapevines will not only serve up succulent fruit, but will reward the gardener with three seasons of beautiful foliage if provided with a trellis to climb.

It is possible to grow blueberries, raspberries, blackberries, currants, and gooseberries in containers, but they require substantial effort and don't tend to add to the aesthetic appeal of the garden. And of course strawberries are easily grown in tall, urn-shaped strawberry jars—a special delight for children (see page 96).

Dwarf fruit tree containers should be at least 12 inches (30cm) deep and filled with a loamy potting soil. The container's confining space will keep trees from becoming too large, but since small containers dry out quickly, the trees must be watered regularly during the entire growing season, and monitored to avoid becoming completely dried out during their dormancy. Most dwarf fruit trees will need to be supported by a stake or trellis.

Tender fruit trees like citrus, pomegranate, and fig will need winter protection from frost and freezing. Even the hardiest trees should be protected from cold winds because roots in small pots are vulnerable to damage, and death, from the cold.

Apple, crab apple, pear, and cherry trees are especially beautiful when grown in a large tub or raised bed and espaliered against a wall or fence. Though requiring a good deal of effort, an espaliered fruit tree is a work of art lending a note of grace and formality to a garden. They also take up much less space than standard-grown fruit trees.

When selecting fruit trees to grow in containers, look for varieties that are hardier than normally required for your climate. This way, they will be better able to withstand the lower temperatures their roots will experience due to being above ground. Also take extra care to protect an espaliered tree in cold regions. The wall will provide some extra warmth, but you might also consider wrapping it in burlap, bubble-wrap, or heavy plastic.

Here are a few varieties of fruit trees that are especially suitable for growing in containers:

❧ Meyer and ponderosa lemons (*Citrus limon* 'Meyer' and *C. l.* 'Ponderosa')—dwarf lemons.

❧ Persian lime (*Citrus aurantifolia* 'Tahiti')—dwarf lime with full-size fruit.

❧ Pomegranate (*Punica granatum* 'Wonderful')—grown as a shrub with bright, sweet, red fruits.

❧ Apple ('Garden Delicious')—an extra dwarf tree, it will grow to only 5 or 6 feet (1.5 or 1.8m), but will bear full-size fruits.

❧ Peach ('Garden Sun')—ideal for containers and growing only to 4 to 5 feet (1.2 to 1.5m).

Vegetables

There is something immeasurably satisfying about growing one's own food. Tending a kitchen garden crammed with ripe vegetables may well be one of life's most delightful activities, but every bit as delectable is growing vegetables in pots on a balcony, deck, fire escape, windowsill, or rooftop.

The key to success with pot-grown vegetables is the depth of the container—9 inches (23cm) is the minimum, and deeper than that is better. Adequate moisture and fertilizer are essential, and a full day of sun is required. If you can meet all these needs, you can grow wonderful vegetables.

Some vegetable varieties are more suitable to pot culture than others. Among the easiest to grow are tomatoes (especially patio varieties), sweet or hot peppers, lettuce, watercress, eggplant, peas, beans, and onions. But the truly determined container gardener will grow just about any vegetable. Oversize tubs, raised beds, and wooden planters can substitute for a large plot in which to grow cucumbers, oriental vegetables, and broccoli, even squash, beets, and corn.

Look for appropriate cultivars in seed catalogs and at garden centers.

TOP: *Yellow cherry tomatoes 'Yellow Canary' make excellent container plants, especially where limited space is a consideration. The cherry varieties are sometimes called patio tomatoes.*

BOTTOM: *A few leaf lettuces, some parsley, and a pair of marguerites in a terracotta bowl would be a wonderful introduction to gardening for a small child. It's manageable, edible, and pretty. A salad garden in a dish is actually ideal for anyone with the desire to grow vegetables without a great deal of effort.*

～ Ornamental Grasses ～

Blue, golden, and variegated grasses grown in simple earthen pots suggest a contemporary or oriental character. The gardener has dozens of varieties from which to choose, including some hardy varieties like Glyceria maxima *'Variegata',* Hordeum jubatum *(squirreltail barley),* Heliototrichon sempervirens *(blue oat grass),* Carex elata *'Aurea' (golden sedge),* Miscanthus sinensis *'Gracillimus' (maiden grass),* M. s. *'Zebrinus' (zebra grass), and* Spartina pectinata *'Aureo Marginata' (variegated prairie cord grass).*

The appeal of growing ornamental grasses is increasing as gardeners discover their useful qualities. Whether tall or diminutive, they add structure and architectural interest to a container garden, along with a wide range of color and shape. And because grasses often dry attractively, their contribution in winter can be considerable.

There are many ornamental grasses suitable for pots. Here are a few especially attractive ones:

❧ Blue fescue (*Festuca ovina*)—Growing in neat clumps of fine 10- to 24-inch (25 to 60cm) thin leaves, fescue varieties cover a range of steely blues and will grow in sun or light shade and tolerate dry conditions.

❧ Pampas grass (*Cortaderia selloana*)—Look for a dwarf variety like 'Pumila' of this spectacular grass to grow in a massive terra-cotta pot. Three-foot (90cm)-long, thin, green leaves cascade from the plant's center. In late summer, feathery beige plumes up to 6 feet (1.8m) tall tower above. The plumes will dry, holding up through the winter if protected from the wind. Cut them back in the spring.

❧ Hardy clump bamboo (*Fargesia murielae*)—Fine green foliage on 8- to 12-foot (2.4 to 3.7m) stems, this tough bamboo is useful for screening or providing shade. Grow it in a permanent planter or an oversize tub.

❧ Fountain grass (*Pennisetum alopecuroides*)—Deep green, 3-foot (90cm)-tall narrow leaves grow in tight clumps and produce tall silvery brown plumes in midsummer through fall. The spiky plumes will last all winter.

❧ *Miscanthus sinensis*—This is an entire family of beautiful ornamental grasses including *M. s. purpurescens* or 'flame grass', which turns a red-orange in the fall and *M. s.* 'Strictus', or 'porcupine grass', with horizontal yellow stripes on its bright green leaves.

Plants for Fragrance

Fragrance is sometimes overlooked in garden planning. Yet smell is among the most highly developed of our five senses. Fragrant plants perfume the air, evoking fond memories or setting a romantic mood.

One of the beauties of planting in containers is the flexibility it gives the gardener. One of the most delightful blessings of being able to move plants around is placing a particularly fragrant flower in an advantageous spot when it comes into bloom.

To add lovely scent to your garden, fill a few pots with some of the plants listed here, and place them near an open window, on the terrace where you often sit, or along a garden path where you enjoy a quiet stroll. In a small garden, especially one with perimeter walls or fences, scents can become quite concentrated. Experiment with the fragrances you enjoy most, and avoid those that conflict with each other.

Lilies (*Lillium*)—Among the most regal of flowers, lilies, particularly the oriental and Asiatic varieties, are as highly fragrant as they are showy. Especially perfumed are 'Casa Blanca', specium 'Rubrum', and 'Star Gazer'. 'Sans Souci',

'Little Pink', 'Little Girl', and 'Gold Band' are shorter varieties, making them ideal for growing in pots. Because lilies need full sun, but like to have their roots kept cool, add low-growing plants like thyme, lobelia, ivy geranium, or dwarf plumbago at their feet. And as lilies are not known for their foliage, plan to keep them in an out-of-the-way place until they are ready to bloom. Then, once their show is over, move them back to the wings. It's a fair amount of effort, but the heavenly scent, along with their outstanding beauty, is well worth the effort.

Daylilies (*Hemerocallis*)—While most daylilies aren't meant for pot culture, 'Stella d'Oro' is. A diminutive variety, growing to about 2 feet (60cm), 'Stella' blooms all summer beginning in June, bringing an intense fragrance with its golden-yellow flowers. 'Mary Todd', 'Hyperion', and 'Lexington' are also known for scent and will adapt to growing in containers.

Amazon lily (*Eucharis grandiflora*)—Not technically a lily, this summer-flowering bulb has fragrant white flowers most of the summer.

Scented geranium (*Pelargonium*)—The dozens of varieties of pelargoniums have scents ranging from rose and mint to chocolate and apple, and include orange, ginger, cinnamon, and coconut. They are easy to grow, and though their flowers are insignificant, the scented foliage blends in well with other plants.

Lily of the valley (*Convallaria majalis*)—These tiny sprays of white bells have an intense perfume in midspring. They flourish in shady, moist conditions. The attractive, bright green tuliplike leaves will die back in midsummer, so add a leafy companion plant to cover up the blank spots.

Autumn-blooming clematis (*Clematis paniculata*)—The tiny star-shaped white flowers on this easy-to-grow deciduous vine smell just like honey. Grow it in a big tub or wooden planter placed against a wall or fence with a trellis or wires to climb. Clematis also like to keep their heads in the sun and their feet in the shade, so mulch thickly or grow a dense groundcover in the tub.

Dwarf Korean spice bush (*Viburnum carlesii*)—Be sure to select a dwarf variety or you'll have an 8-foot-(2.4m) wide shrub to deal with. Highly perfumed white flowers appear in May.

Fragrant annuals like nicotiana, sweet alyssum, dianthus varieties, sweet peas, morning glories, moonflower, heliotrope, and common stock can all be successfully pot-grown.

Other fragrant plants to grow in pots include roses, lavender, jasmine, azaleas, gardenia, violets, hyacinths, tuberoses, and bay.

Foliage Plants

While flowering plants tend to be the glamorous stars of the potted garden, foliage plants fill essential supporting roles. Often, when the grand spectacle of blooms has passed, a foliage plant will step in as the understudy, effectively stealing the show.

Gertrude Jekyll used foliage plants extensively, often placing hosta, which she called funkia, in rectangular terra-cotta pots against a wall in a paved court, pairing them with ferns, and added aspidistra and lilies when they were in bloom. She wrote, "The two or three sorts of foliage are in themselves delightful to the eye; often there is nothing with them but lilies, and one hardly desires to have more."

Penelope Hobhouse, in her expert treatise on color, wrote, "Foliage plants shape a garden and establish its structure."

Innumerable shades of green, from chartreuse to deep blue-green, and colored effects like stipples, speckles, stripes, variegation, and veins introduce color, variety, texture, and contrast to the garden. Here are some of the most reliable and rewarding foliage plants for pots.

Hosta

At home in nearly every shade garden, hostas are among the most widely cultivated foliage plants.

Forming clumps of heart-shaped or oval leaves, hostas adapt well to pot culture and will continue to grow and prosper for years, requiring little care. They prefer moist soil, rich in organic matter. They will grow in sun, but prefer shade (an absolute must in hot climates). Hostas produce lavender or white flowers, some highly fragrant, on tall stalks in late summer.

Blue-green varieties include *Hosta sieboldiana* 'Elegans' with rounded, puckered leaves, growing up to 24 inches (60cm) high, and tolerating dry shade; *H.* x *tardiana* 'Halcyon' with heart-shaped, heavily veined leaves, growing 12 inches (30cm) tall; and 'Fragrant Blue' with pale blue rounded leaves, growing only 8 to 12 inches (20 to 30cm) tall.

Chartreuse varieties range from the very large *Hosta* 'Sum and Substance' and *H.* 'Solar Fire', which grow up to 3 feet (90cm) high, to the diminutive *H.* 'Little Aurora', which reaches only 6 inches (15cm) in height.

Variegated varieties include *Hosta* 'So Sweet', with bright green leaves bordered in white, *H.* 'Northern Exposure', bearing blue-green puckered leaves with wide cream margins, and the very popular *H.* 'Francee', whose forest green leaves are edged in white.

Ferns

The feathery, light, and seemingly delicate foliage of ferns is a wonderful foil for the more solid forms of containers. Use them to add texture, soften the hard edges of angular spaces, cover unsightly aspects, give volume to a hanging container, fill in a blank place where another plant display has passed its prime, or make a lush display in a conservatory or on a terrace.

Ferns tend to prefer slightly acid, humusy soil, regular watering, and a location in shade or partial shade. Full sun will burn them. Many ferns are extremely winter-hardy, but some will need to be brought indoors when the winters are cold. Be sure to keep humidity levels high when growing ferns indoors.

Here are some of the best ferns to grow:

Maidenhair fern (*Adiantum pedatum*), one of the most recognizable ferns, has bright green 12- to 20-inch (30 to 51cm) fronds on black stems, and will grow in bright light as long as it is kept out of direct sun. This is not a hardy fern, and must be brought inside when the temperature drops below 50°F (10°C).

Ostrich fern (*Matteuccia pensylvanica*) can become a pest when set free in a garden bed, but when contained in a pot, its 4- to 6-foot (1.2 to 1.8m) fronds make an elegant screen or a background for colorful blooms. Ostrich ferns will grow in full sun, but the bright leaves will turn brown by August.

Christmas fern (*Polystichum acrostichoides*) is one of the few hardy evergreen ferns, making it a valuable addition to the potted garden. Often used in flower arrangements, the 2- to 3-foot (60 to 90cm) dark green fronds have a leathery appearance.

Japanese painted fern (*Athyrium niponicum pictum*) is a delicate beauty with silvery gray-green 2-foot (60cm) fronds on burgundy stems. Filtered sun adds to their coloration. This is an early fern to unfold, so it is a very good companion for spring bulbs.

Variegated holly fern (*Arachniodes simplicior variegata*) is, as its name implies, a variegated fern with a distinct yellow-green stripe running the length of the bright green fronds.

Silver and Gray Foliage

Silver and gray foliage are as valuable in the potted garden as they are in the border garden, bringing with them a soft focus and serving as a visual transition for contrasting colors. Plants to grow in pots for their attractive silver or gray foliage include lamb's ear, artemisia, santolina, lamium (useful in hanging baskets), thyme, sage, rosemary, hebe, Jerusalem sage, tree germander, and lavender.

Other foliage plants to grow in pots include:

Polka-dot plant (*Hypoestes*)—White or pink-dotted oval leaves add a playful touch to containers in sun or partial shade. These tender plants look beautiful alone or when combined with New Guinea impatiens, begonias, coleus, or ferns.

Coleus (sometimes called painted nettle)—One of the most common potted plants for shade, coleus has been snubbed by many a contemporary gardener for its old-fashioned nature, but it deserves renewed attention. Combine the patterned red, maroon, chartreuse, green, white, and pink coleus with ferns or impatiens. Or tuck them in as underplantings for large green houseplants which are summering outdoors.

Caladium—These tender bulbs feature heart-shaped leaves with exotic colorations: bright red with red margins, pale green with raspberry-colored speckles, pale pink with heavy green veining, or silvery white with red veins. The gigantic "elephant ear" caladium, although all green, is

one of the showiest foliage plants you can have in your garden. All caladiums are very easy to grow and are spectacular in a cast-iron urn, an ornamented cement planter, or a wicker planter.

Begonia—Often valued more for their blooms, there are dozens of begonia varieties with handsome, exotic, and colorful foliage. *Begonia rex* (pink, rough, variegated), *B. semperflorens* (shiny, leathery, dark green), and *B. coccinea* (angel-wing) are three useful varieties.

Tender plants grown indoors, like philodendron, clivia, streptocarpus, abuliton, dieffenbachia, schefflera, dracaena, ficus, cordyline, and various palms, will often prosper from a summer spent outside on a terrace, balcony, or deck, where their diverse foliage will serve as a backdrop for other potted plants, or as points of interest in their own right. Most, however, will need protection from the summer sun.

See the section on trees and shrubs in this chapter (pages 100–102) for other plants useful for their foliage.

Suggested Reading

Allen, Oliver E. *Gardening with the New Small Plants*. Boston: Houghton Mifflin Company, 1987. Essential information about dwarf conifers, rhododendrons, azaleas, alpines, vegetables, perennials, and annuals.

Bayard, Tania. *Gardening for Fragrance*. New York: Brooklyn Botanic Garden, 1989. A small booklet crammed with information about scented plants.

Beckett, Kenneth A., David Carr, and David Stevens. *The Contained Garden*. New York: Viking, 1982. Extensive information on care and maintenance including pests and diseases.

Brennan, Georgeanne. *Fragrant Flowers*. San Francisco: Chronicle Books, 1994. Part of the same series as the next two books, this one has great ideas about fragrance.

Brennan, Georgeanne, and Mimi Luebbermann. *Beautiful Bulbs*. San Francisco: Chronicle Books, 1993. An entire book of practical information about growing bulbs in containers.

———. *Little Herb Gardens*. San Francisco: Chronicle Books, 1993. Three chapters on growing herbs in pots and other containers.

Brickell, C. *Pruning Roses, Deciduous Shrubs, Evergreens, Hedges, All Shrubs, Fruit Bushes and Trees, Deciduous Trees*. New York: Simon & Schuster, 1979. Everything you'll need to know about pruning.

Brookes, John. *The Small Garden Book*. New York: Crown Publishers, Inc., 1989. Innovative ways to get the most garden from the least space.

Bryan, Lynn. *Conservatory Gardening*. Sydney, Australia: Lansdowne Publishing, 1993. Good ideas for indoor gardening.

Dillon, Helen. *The Flower Garden*. New York: Sterling Publishing Company, Inc., 1995. From the Wayside Garden Collection. Although not focused on container gardening, the basics are covered and the pictures are lovely.

Druse, Ken. *Water Gardening*. New York: Prentice-Hall, 1993. Straightforward instructions, more for larger water gardens than those in tubs. Good list of water plants.

Ferguson, Barbara. *Color with Annuals*. San Francisco: Ortho Books, 1987. Helpful lists of annuals.

Gibson, Michael. *Growing Roses*. Portland, Oreg.: Timber Press, 1984. A good, basic rose book with excellent varietal descriptions.

———. *Growing Roses for Small Gardens*. Portland, Oreg.: Timber Press, 1990. Extensive survey of roses, many of which can be grown in containers.

Harper, Pamela J. *Color Echos*. New York: Macmillan Publishing Company, 1994. How to create color harmony in the garden.

Heriteau, Jacqueline. *The National Arboretum Book of Outstanding Garden Plants*. New York: Simon & Schuster, 1990. An encyclopedia of 106 categories of plants including trees for color, foliage, or fragrance; vines for shade; grasses for sunny, dry urban areas.

Hobhouse, Penelope. *Color in Your Garden*. Boston: Little, Brown and Company, 1985. Expert advice from a superb garden colorist.

———. *Gardening Through the Ages*. New York: Simon & Schuster, 1992. Everything you've ever wanted to know about the history of gardening by one of the twentieth century's greatest gardeners. Beautifully illustrated.

———. *On Gardening*. New York: Macmillan, 1994. Invaluable information for the plant person.

Holmes, Roger, ed. *Taylor's Guide to Container Gardening*. Boston: Houghton Mifflin Company, 1995. Helpful for its encyclopedia of three hundred plants to use in pots.

Jekyll, Gertrude. *Colour in the Flower Garden*. Reprint, Portland, Oreg.: Timber Press, 1995. A reissue of the classic book on color originally published in 1908.

Jones, David L. *Enclopedia of Ferns*. Portland, Oreg.: Timber Press, 1987). Essential botanical and cultural information.

Kohlein, Fritz, and Peter Menzel. *Color Encyclopedia of Garden Plants and Habitats*. Portland, Oreg.: Timber Press, 1994. An impressive survey of what grows where.

Nick, Jean M.A., and Fern Marshall Bradley. *Growing Fruits & Vegetables Organically*. Emmaus, Pa.: Rodale Press, 1994. Solid, basic information with a chapter on container gardening.

Organic Gardening magazine editors. *Best Methods for Growing Fruits and Berries*. Emmaus, Pa.: Rodale Press, Inc., 1981. A practical guide to growing fruit with a chapter on strawberries in containers.

Robinson, Peter. *The Water Garden*. New York: Sterling Publishing Company, Inc., 1995. From the Wayside Garden Collection. An especially good source of information on aquatic plants.

Rogers, Allan. *Peonies*. Portland, Ore.: Timber Press, Inc., 1995. Everything you've ever wanted to know about growing peonies.

Sackville-West, Vita. V. *Sackville-West's Garden Book*. New York: Atheneum, 1983. A newer edition of a collection of Vita's breezy and informative newspaper columns originally compiled by her son Nigel Nicolson in 1968.

Schmid, W. Geroge. *The Genus Hosta*. Portland, Oreg.: Timber Press, 1992. A comprehensive look at hostas.

Sunset Books editors. *Vegetable Gardening Illustrated*. Menlo Park, Calif.: Lane Publishing Co., 1987. Straightforward, how-to information for growing vegetables and small fruits with good sections on raised beds and container gardening.

Tarling, Thomasina. *The Container Garden*. New York: Sterling Publishing Co., Inc., 1994. From the Wayside Garden Collection, this is a practical guide to planning and planting.

Verey, Rosemary. *Rosemary Verey's Garden Plans*. London: Frances Lincoln Publishers, 1993. Worth looking at for the pictures alone, and lots of nicely planted containers.

Wilkinson, Elizabeth, and Marjorie Henderson, eds. *Decorating Eden*. San Francisco: Chronicle Books, 1992. A comprehensive sourcebook of classic garden details.

Yang, Linda. *The City Gardener's Handbook*. New York: Random House, 1990. Great advice for city gardeners.

———. *The Terrace Gardener's Handbook*. Beaverton, Oreg.: Timber Press, 1982. No-nonsense approach to the special needs of terrace gardening.

Sources
Pots and Containers

Five O Seven Antiques
507 King Street East
Toronto, Ontario M5A 1M3, Canada
(416) 891-1273
Antique cast iron, stone, lead, and terra-cotta garden containers.

Hobensack & Keller
Bridge Street
New Hope, PA 18938
(215) 862-2406
A large collection of antique and reproduction cast iron, lead, marble dust, marble chip, cast cement, hand-pressed sandstone, cast aluminum and bronze planters, urns, pots, vases, wire plant stands, and other containers.

Kinsman Company
River Road, Dept. 225
Point Pleasant, PA 18950
(800) 733-5613
An extensive catalog selection of wire hay racks, planters, wall and hanging baskets, hooks, liners, freestanding wire planters, troughs, and circular planters.

The Romantic Garden Nursery
The Street, Swannington
Norwich, Norfolk, England
011-01-6032-61488
Frost-proof Italian terra-cotta pots, topiaries, and plants for the conservatory.

Smith & Hawkin
25 Corte Madera
Mill Valley, CA 94941
(415) 383-2000
Teak planters and window boxes and terra-cotta pots.

Tennessee Fabricating Company
1822 Latham Street
Memphis, TN 38106
(901) 948-3356
Cast iron and cast aluminum Victorian reproduction patterns.

Whichford Pottery
Whichford near Shipston-on-Stour
Warwickshire, England
011-02-6086-84416
Hand-thrown, guaranteed frost-proof terra-cotta pots in enormous range of styles and sizes.

Plants and Seeds

The Cook's Garden
P.O. Box 535
Londonderry, VT 05148
(802)824-3400
Seed for culinary plants with an especially large collection of herbs.

The Fragrant Path
P.O. Box 328
Fort Calhoun, NE 68023
Mail order seeds for fragrant, rare, and old-fashioned plants.

Geo. W. Park Seed Co., Inc.
Cokesbury Road
Greenwood, SC 29647-0001
(864)223-7333
Mail order flower and vegetable seeds, herbs, fruit plants, perennial plants.

Thompson & Morgan
P.O. Box 1308
Jackson, NJ 08527
(800) 274-733 / (908) 363-2225
The famous English mail order seed company.

W. Atlee Burpee & Co.
Warminister, PA 18974
(800) 888-1447
Mail order flower and vegetable seeds, bulbs, herbs, and perennial plants.

Wayside Gardens
Hodges, SC 29695
(800) 845-1124
A popular mail order company.

Trees and Shrubs
Eastern Plant Specialties
Box 226
Georgetown, ME 04548
(207) 371-2888
Mail order nursery.

Imperatore Nursery
Windy Bush Road
New Hope, PA 18938
(215) 598-7882
Japanese maples, dwarfed lodge pole pine, and mountain hemlock in large wooden containers. Wholesale only.

Fruit Trees
Henry Leuthardt Nurseries, Inc.
Montauk Highway
Box 666
East Moriches, NY 11940
(516) 878-1387
Old varieties of apples, pears, peaches, plums, and grapes, including dwarf, semi-dwarf, and espalier trees.

Stark Bros.
Highway 54
Louisiana, MO 63353
(314)754-4525
A big selection of mail order fruit trees.

Bulbs
The Daffodil Mart
7463 Heath Trail
Gloucester, VA 23061
(800) ALL-BULB
Mail order bulbs including 187 varieties of daffodils.

Dutch Gardens
P.O. Box 200
Adelphia, NJ 07710
(908) 780-2713
OR
Vennestraat
2160 AA Lisse-Holand
011-31-2521-14648
Mail order bulbs with thick, full-color catalogs for spring and fall-bloomers.

Water Plants
Discount Pond Supplies
P.O. Box 423371
Kissimmee, FL 34742
(407) 847-7937
Water gardening supplies and aquatic plants by mail order.

Japonica
36484 Camp Creek Road
Springfield, OR 97478
Mail order water lilies, bog plants, lotus.

Horticultural Societies
The American Horticultural Society
7931 East Boulevard Drive
Alexandria, VA 22308
(703) 768-5700

The American Rose Society
P.O. Box 30000
Shreveport, LA 71130
(318) 938-5402

The Garden Club of America
598 Madison Avenue
New York, NY 10022
(212) 753-8287

Herb Society of America, Inc.
9019 Kirtland Chardon
Mentor, OH 44060
(216) 256-0514

Index